r T   We Hate

Freedom for the Thought That We Hate

✧ ✧ ✧

A Biography of the First Amendment

ANTHONY LEWIS

BASIC
BOOKS

A Member of the Perseus Books Group
New York

Designed by Brent Wilcox

The Library of Congress has cataloged the hardcover as follows:
Lewis, Anthony, 1927-
  Freedom for the thought that we hate : a biography of the First
Amendment / Anthony Lewis.
       p. cm.
  Includes bibliographical references and index.
  ISBN-13: 978-0-465-03917-3 (alk. paper)
  ISBN-10: 0-465-03917-0 (alk. paper)
  1. Freedom of speech--United States. 2. Freedom of the press--
United States. I. Title.

  KF4770.L49 2007
  342.7308'53--dc22

                                                    2007040249
Paperback ISBN: 978-0-465-01819-2

10 9 8 7 6 5 4 3 2 1

To Margie
Who makes everything possible

CONTENTS

Introduction   ix

1 Beginnings   1
2 "Odious or Contemptible"   11
3 "As All Life Is an Experiment"   23
4 Defining Freedom   39
5 Freedom and Privacy   59
6 A Press Privilege?   81
7 Fear Itself   101
8 "Another's Lyric"   131
9 "Vagabonds and Outlaws"   143
10 Thoughts That We Hate   157
11 Balancing Interests   169
12 Freedom of Thought   183

Acknowledgments   191
Table of Cases   193
Notes   197
Index   209

INTRODUCTION

Ours is the most outspoken society on earth. Americans are freer to think what we will and say what we think than any other people, and freer today than in the past. We can bare the secrets of government and the secrets of the bedroom. We can denounce our rulers, and each other, with little fear of the consequences. There is almost no chance that a court will stop us from publishing what we wish: in print, on the air, or on the Web. Hateful and shocking expression, political or artistic, is almost all free to enter the marketplace of ideas.

Other countries that we think of as like our own—Britain, for example—have many more restrictions on what can be said. Why are we different? Where does our extraordinary freedom come from? The answer commonly given is "the First Amendment." That amendment to the United States Constitution provides, among other things, that "Congress shall make no law . . . abridging the freedom of speech, or of the press. . . . "

But those fourteen words cannot in themselves account for our great freedom, because over many decades they did not protect critical expression. In 1798, just seven years after the

First Amendment was added to the Constitution, Congress passed a law that punished disrespectful comment on the president; editors were imprisoned for mocking President John Adams. A century later, under another congressional statute, men were sentenced to twenty years in prison for criticizing a policy decision by President Woodrow Wilson.

Today every president is the target of criticism and mockery. It is inconceivable that even the most caustic critic would be imprisoned for his or her words. If such a prosecution were attempted, the courts would throw it out as in conflict with the First Amendment. So something has happened to the fourteen words of the speech and press clauses. Their meaning has changed. Or, more accurately, the understanding of those words has changed: judges' understanding and the public's.

To say that is to open the way to appreciating a mysterious and remarkable process: the changing interpretation of our fundamental law. "We are under a Constitution," Chief Justice Charles Evans Hughes said, "but the Constitution is what the judges say it is." That may sound today like a cynical description of what critics on the Right call "judicial activism." But Hughes, who said it in 1907, three years before he was first appointed to the Supreme Court, thought he was stating the obvious. Someone has to interpret the words of our eighteenth-century Constitution and its amendments; under our system as it has developed, that is the job of the courts.

Judges do not operate in a vacuum. They are influenced by the attitudes of their society, and the society in turn may be influenced by what the courts say. So history, law, and culture contribute to the process of defining what the Constitution commands.

When we say today that the First Amendment guarantees our freedom, we mean not only its brief text but the vast body of law that judges have built up over the years in applying it to issues brought before them. When a dissident burns the flag to protest official policy, is that a form of expression protected by the First Amendment? Is political campaign spending immune from regulation as protected "speech"? What about a false and damaging attack on a politician: Can he or she collect damages for libel?

In answering such questions, courts look to what earlier judges have said on more or less analogous issues. Each decision becomes a precedent for others. It is called the "common-law method," because for centuries, English and then American judges built up the rules of property, contracts, and the like in what was called the "common law": law defined not by explicit statutes but by judicial decisions.

The defining of our fundamental laws in this way is a drama, and nowhere more so than in the law of the First Amendment. It has been a drama since 1791, and it still is today: a tale without end. First Amendment law poses hard questions, for judges and the rest of us. How unregulated a society do we really want? Where should the line be drawn between liberty and order? Is the demand for "no law" abridging the freedom of speech and press an absolute? Those are some of the questions I shall discuss in this book as I explore the meaning of the First Amendment in law and society.

The story of the First Amendment is powerful testimony to the crucial role of judges in a political system that rests on a foundation of law. Voters are the ultimate sovereigns in a republic, as James Madison and the other Framers of the Constitution said. But transient political majorities cannot be expected to articulate the fundamental values of a constitution, least of all when the majority's immediate interest conflicts with those values—as, from time to time, it will. Judges, serving for long terms and bound by their commissions to look beyond momentary partisan conflicts, are in the best position to give voice to the deeper values.

So the American experience teaches. Until World War II it was a uniquely American practice to give courts, especially the Supreme Court, a significant role in the structure of governance. No other democratic society had a constitution enforced by judges. In Britain and its empire, the doctrine of parliamentary supremacy prevailed; whatever a parliament did—however discriminatory, however unjust—was law. But the tyrannies of the twentieth century brought a change.

Aharon Barak, then the president of the Israeli Supreme Court, explained the change in a 1998 lecture. In the past, he said, people thought that respect for basic values "could be guaranteed by relying on the self-restraint of the majority." But after the Nazis, the lesson was that there must be "formal limits on the power of the majority. The concept that 'It is not done' needs to receive the formal expression, 'It is forbidden.'"

And so, country after country adopted *constitutional* democracy, giving the last word to judges on basic issues. That was the pattern in a state with as profound a republican system as

France, and then in a reconstructed Germany. It was followed in the great former British territories, notably India and South Africa. And the countries of Europe adopted a European Convention on Human Rights, enforced by a Court of Human Rights. In time, even Britain agreed that its own courts should be bound by the European Convention.

As the history of the First Amendment shows, putting a guarantee into a charter is no assurance that it will be enforced. After all, it took more than a century for the courts to begin protecting dissenting speakers and publishers from official repression in the United States. Or to put it another way, it took time for judges to build on the fundamental promise of those fourteen words in the First Amendment: that this would be a country of free speech and freedom of the press. Time and imagination and courage. Timid, unimaginative judges could not have made America as extraordinarily free as it is.

Freedom to speak and write as you wish is the inescapable necessity of democracy. The judges of the European Court of Human Rights understood that when, in 1986, they considered the right to criticize political leaders. They did not consider the issue in a vacuum; they built on American experience and decisions.

An Austrian journalist, Peter Michael Lingens, had written articles charging a politician with the "basest opportunism." The politician sued for libel, and the Austrian courts awarded him damages. Lingens went to the European Court of Human Rights, which found that the libel judgment against him violated the Convention on Human Rights—its clause guaranteeing freedom of expression. That freedom, the court said, "constitutes one of the essential foundations of a democratic society. . . . It is applicable not only to 'information' or 'ideas' that are favorably received or regarded as inoffensive . . . but also to those that offend, shock or disturb. Such are the demands of that pluralism, tolerance and broadmindedness without which there is no 'democratic society.'" In other words, as Justice Oliver Wendell Holmes Jr. of the United States Supreme Court said, "freedom for the thought that we hate."

When a constitutional provision has no discernible history, as is true of the First Amendment—no meaningful discussion by its authors of what they meant—how do judges begin to build on its words to decide concrete cases? That is a subject of endless debate. But one thing is sure. Judges, however bold, are part of their society and are influenced by its attitudes. To give a stark example: The Nazi experience made more Americans, and judges, understand the devastating character of religious and racial discrimination.

Justice Ruth Bader Ginsburg of the Supreme Court, speaking at the University of Cape Town, South Africa, in 2006, said: "What caused the Court's understanding to dawn and grow? Judges do read newspapers and are affected, not by the weather of the day, as distinguished constitutional law professor Paul Freund once said, but by the climate of the era."

Justice Ginsburg was talking about gender discrimination. But her point applies to the drama of the First Amendment's expanding interpretation since early in the twentieth century. Great judges like Holmes saw, before most judges and most Americans, that freedom of thought was an essential element in the success of our diverse society. But judicial commitment to openness of expression grew as citizens' did; each informed the other. And it is worth remembering that the 1798 statute criminalizing criticism of the president, which was enforced by judges, was rejected by American voters in the election of 1800 as incompatible with the First Amendment and with American ideals.

The meaning of the First Amendment has been, and will be, shaped by each American generation: by judges, political leaders, citizens. There will always be authorities who try to make their own lives more comfortable by suppressing critical comment. There will always be school principals like the one in Wilton, Connecticut, who in 2007 canceled a student play about the war in Iraq because it might disturb some families. But I am convinced that the fundamental American commitment to free speech, disturbing speech, is no longer in doubt.

1

Beginnings

The American commitment to freedom of speech and press is the more remarkable because it emerged from legal and political origins that were highly repressive. The colonists who crossed the Atlantic in the seventeenth century came from an England where it was extremely dangerous to utter a thought that differed from official truth. The state defined what was allowable in politics and, perhaps even more rigorously, in religion.

Repression was accomplished by two different devices. The first was preventive: a licensing system for all publications. In England in 1538, King Henry VIII issued a proclamation requiring anyone who wanted to print something to get a license first. The requirement applied to everything: books (Bibles were the biggest seller), pamphlets, shipping schedules. The system created valuable printing monopolies, and it prevented the publication of unorthodox opinions.

The licensers were bureaucrats who operated with utter arbitrariness. They took as long as they wished to decide whether something could be printed, and they gave no reasons for their decisions. When they said no, there was no appeal. This system of previous restraints on publication, as they were called, provoked the classic protest against censorship, by the poet and essayist John Milton: "Areopagitica—A Speech for the Liberty of Unlicensed Printing."

When Parliament overthrew King Charles I in the civil war of the 1640s, it abolished the royal licensing system. But as is so often the case, the rebels became less tolerant of dissent when they exercised power. In 1643 Parliament enacted its own licensing statute. It lasted until 1694, when Parliament let it die by failing to renew the law.

The second repressive device may have been even more intimidating. It was the law of seditious libel, which made it a crime to publish anything disrespectful of the state or church or their officers. The premise of seditious libel was that these institutions had to have respect for the country to avoid the terrible danger of social chaos. If you published something critical—a charge, say, that an official had taken a bribe—it did you no good to prove that the statement was true. Truth was no defense to a charge of seditious libel. The crime lay in reducing public respect for the official, so a truthful criticism might be even worse than a false one. A defendant was entitled to trial by jury, but the judge alone (appointed by the state) decided whether the publication was seditious; the jury considered only whether the defendant had published it. Punishment upon conviction included the death penalty, carried out by the lingering horror of being hanged, drawn, and quartered.

Curiously, from our viewpoint today, critics of the licensing system often did not object to the rigors of subsequent punishment. "It is of greatest concernment in the Church and Commonwealth," Milton wrote, "to have a vigilant eye how books demean themselves as well as men: and therefore to confine, imprison, and do sharpest justice on them as malefactors."

Sir William Blackstone was the leading authority on the common law, including seditious libel. Like Milton, he drew a sharp distinction between it and prior restraint by licensing. "Where blasphemous, immoral, treasonable, schismatical, seditious or scandalous libels are punished by the English law," he wrote in 1769,

> the liberty of the press, properly understood, is by no means infringed or violated. . . . [It] consists in laying no *previous* restraints upon publications, and not in freedom from censure for criminal matter when published. . . . To punish (as the law does at present) any dangerous or offensive writings, which, when published, shall on a fair and impartial trial be adjudged of a pernicious tendency, is necessary for the preservation of peace and good order, a government and religion, the only solid foundations of civil liberty.

Blackstone's eminence notwithstanding, there was not much protection in his talk of a "fair and impartial trial" when judges relied on the slippery concept of "a pernicious tendency" to decide whether something was seditious and truth was not a defense.

Colonial America began with little tolerance of dissent. Puritans crossed the ocean for freedom to practice their religion, but they did not extend that freedom to others. Massachusetts hanged Mary Dyer in 1660 because she insisted on advocating her Quaker views. Colonial judges applied the common law of England, including the law of seditious libel. But the public began, after a time, to resist. That was the lesson of the first great legal test of press freedom in America, the case of John Peter Zenger.

Zenger was a New York printer. He printed—though he had nothing to do with the content—a newspaper, the *New-York Weekly Journal*, that attacked the royal governor of New York, William Cosby. Cosby had Zenger prosecuted for seditious libel. At his trial in 1735 Zenger's lawyer, Andrew Hamilton of Philadelphia, argued that the criticisms of Governor Cosby in the newspaper were accurate. That was irrelevant under seditious libel law, as Hamilton knew—truth was not a defense. The judge, a Cosby appointee, so ruled. But Hamilton appealed to the jurors to ignore the judge's ruling, make up their own minds, and free Zenger if they found the newspaper's criticisms of Cosby to be true. The jury found Zenger not guilty: an extraordinary decision that could not formally change the law but that reverberated around the colonies and discouraged further prosecutions for seditious libel.

The newspapers of eighteenth-century America were raggle-taggle affairs, nothing like the highly capitalized metropolitan press known to us. Anyone could put out a newspaper by bringing the copy to a job printer like Peter Zenger. The papers were highly partisan, the editors often political party men. The *New-York Weekly Journal* that got Zenger in trouble was started and written by a political faction opposed to Governor Cosby. There was little pretense of objectivity. Even a figure as lofty as George Washington was not above rancid criticism. When he retired from the presidency in 1797, the *Philadelphia Aurora* called him "the source of all the misfortunes of our country" and said every American heart "ought to beat high with exultation that the name of Washington from this day ceases to give a currency to political iniquity."

In a 1960 book, *Legacy of Suppression*, professor Leonard Levy argued that at the end of the eighteenth century—when the First Amendment was adopted—the much-vaunted liberty of the press in America was freedom only from prior restraint, not from punishment for disapproved words. The law of seditious libel was alive and well then, he said. His book caused a scholarly stir. But twenty-five years later, Levy mostly took it back. In a new edition of the book, retitled *Emergence of a Free Press*, he said further research had shown him that though legal theory remained repressive, in practice "the press conducted itself as if the law scarcely existed." It was highly critical of politicians, indeed "habitually scurrilous."

Prosecutions for seditious libel dwindled in the last decades of the eighteenth century, no doubt in part because the authorities feared they would outrage the public. But as late as 1803 an editor in Hudson, New York, Harry Croswell, was prosecuted in the state courts for an attack on President Thomas Jefferson. The story in his newspaper, *The Wasp*, said that while vice president under John Adams, Jefferson had paid a journalist to write savage assaults on Adams and

Washington. (The journalist called Washington "a traitor, a robber and a perjuror.") Croswell was convicted—but got out of jail when the New York legislature, a year later, made truth a defense against seditious libel charges.

In that turbulent mix of repressive law and an audacious press, the idea arose of committing governments to the principle of press freedom in their fundamental documents. Virginia was the first to act, in 1776. The Declaration of Rights that its colonial legislature adopted in that momentous year included this statement: "The freedom of the press is one of the greatest bulwarks of liberty, and can never be restrained but by despotic Governments." By the time the federal Constitution was drafted in 1787 and the First Amendment added in 1791, nine of the original thirteen states had such provisions in their constitutions or other basic documents.

Writers and printers were no doubt gratified to have their freedom hailed in state constitutions. But what did these provisions actually mean by "the liberty of the press"? Blackstone was highly influential in American courts; and many legal authorities agreed with him that the liberty meant only freedom from prior restraint, not from prosecutions for seditious libel. In that view, the warm words about freedom of the press did not mean much, since prior restraints had died out after England abandoned the licensing system for printing in 1694. Blackstone in effect offered freedom from a restraint that hardly existed any more.

And there was an even more profound doubt about the usefulness of the state calls for freedom of the press. Today we take it for granted that the words of a constitution are enforceable as law, a superior law that in lawsuits can trump current legislation. But that was not the received view in the eighteenth century. Some people did speak of constitutional provisions as legally enforceable. But they were generally thought of as mere admonitions to state legislatures, encouraging but not binding. The phrasing of the press-freedom clause in Virginia's Declaration of Rights, quoted above, certainly sounds more like exhortation than law.

The first time judges enforced a constitutional provision to strike down an established common-law practice occurred in Massachusetts. In 1780, it acquired a constitution, largely drafted by John Adams, that began, "All men are born free and equal." Three years later the Supreme Judicial Court of the commonwealth heard the case of Quock Walker, a Negro slave who said he had been promised his freedom and, when it was not forthcoming, ran away. His master, Nathaniel Jennison, found him and beat him. Jennison was prosecuted for assault and battery. He argued in his defense that slavery was long established in Massachusetts, and he had the right to seize and punish a runaway. But what was the significance of the language about "free and equal"? Chief Justice William Cushing said it was incompatible with slavery, which therefore could "no longer be tolerated." With that, slavery ended in Massachusetts.

The federal Constitution of 1787 had no bill of rights—no guarantee of free speech or press or any other right. But it quickly acquired one under exigent political circumstances. When the Constitution was put to conventions in the states for ratification, opposition was fierce. The opponents included such notable advocates of liberty as Patrick Henry and George Mason of Virginia, who feared that the new federal government would have too much power and could oppress the people.

Conventions in the key states of Massachusetts, New York, and Virginia were leaning against ratification. Then, in Massachusetts, John Hancock came up with a device that persuaded some of the doubters. He proposed that the convention ratify the Constitution and at the same time call on the first Congress elected under it to adopt a bill of rights. With that, the Massachusetts convention voted for ratification, 187 to 168. The New York convention followed, by a vote of 30 to 27, and Virginia's by 89 to 79. By such narrow margins did the United States come into being.

James Madison, a leading figure in the making of the Constitution, opposed the idea of a bill of rights at the time. He feared that listing some specific rights would lead to the view that others, overlooked in the drafting, were not valued. For protection of freedoms he relied on the fact that the Constitution gave only limited, named powers to the new federal government—so it would have no power over matters not mentioned, including the press. And he did not believe that declarations of rights were effective. In a 1788 letter to Jefferson, who was in Paris as the American minister, Madison dismissed what he called "parchment barriers" and said that bills of rights had been repeatedly violated "by overbearing majorities in every State." He was evidently thinking of bills of rights as admonitions to legislatures, not as law enforceable in courts.

(In reply to Madison, Jefferson said there was one argument in favor of a bill of rights that "has great weight with me; the legal check which it puts in the hands of the judiciary." Jefferson was evidently anticipating that the courts would enforce a bill of rights by holding unconstitutional legislation that was inconsistent with its provisions. But when Chief Justice John Marshall, in *Marbury v. Madison* in 1803, found a congressional statute invalid as a violation of the Constitution, Jefferson, now president, fumed that Marshall's decision would "make the judiciary a despotic branch." Consistency was not one of Jefferson's virtues.)

Madison, despite his previous opposition to a bill of rights, pushed for one when he took his seat as a member of the House of Representatives in the first Congress. The contrary view had persuaded him, and perhaps he felt an obligation to carry out the wishes of the key state ratifying conventions. He got twelve constitutional amendments through the House and Senate. What is now the First Amendment was third on the list. The first two, dealing with the number of representatives and congressional salaries, were not approved by the necessary three-fourths of the states. The remaining ten were added to the Constitution on December 15, 1791, when the last needed state, Virginia, ratified them.

Some judges and lawyers argue today that judges should interpret a provision of the Constitution by looking to the "original intention" of its Framers. According to the "Originalists," as they are called, this is to be done by reading statements of the members of Congress who proposed a constitutional amendment, the debates over it, and the comments during the ratification process. But such exploration has little to say about the First Amendment. Madison proposed the idea in the House, the language was changed in committee and in the Senate, and nothing of note was said. Indeed, the Senate then kept no record of its debates. The birth of the First Amendment threw no light on how its scope should be understood. But it was not long before the Constitution and the country underwent a profound test of what was meant by "the freedom of speech, or of the press."

2

"Odious or Contemptible"

On July 4, 1798, the United States Senate passed a bill to make seditious libel a federal crime. Its backers, in the Federalist Party, had chosen the date to identify the legislation with patriotism. The House, also under Federalist control, passed the bill on July 10. President John Adams, a Federalist, signed it into law on July 14. Ten days from start to finish: a swift course for a fateful statute.

The Sedition Act made it a crime to write or publish "any false, scandalous and malicious writing or writings against the government of the United States, or either house of the Congress . . . or the President . . . with intent to defame . . . or to bring them, or either of them, into contempt or disrepute; or to excite against them or either or any of them, the hatred of the good people of the United States." Violators were subject to imprisonment for up to two years and a fine of up to $2,000.

What was the rush in legislating against "sedition"? The law was needed, it was said, to defend the country against terrorism: French terrorism. The French Revolution of 1789 had led to Jacobin Terror and the guillotine. Some Americans, especially those of conservative outlook, feared that France would export its ideology. The French had provided crucial support in the American Revolution, but feelings of gratitude for that faded with the bloody events in Paris.

Fear of French terror was used for a political purpose in the Sedition Act. The party system was just emerging, and the Federalists spoke for what could be called the established forces. The rising opposition, more populist, called themselves Republicans. (Despite the name, they were the ancestors of the modern Democratic Party.) They supported the vice president, Thomas Jefferson. Partisan feelings were fierce. Abigail Adams, the president's wife, wrote a friend in 1798 that "the French party"—the Republicans— were busy "sowing the seeds of vice, irreligion, corruption and sedition."

The Federalists designed the Sedition Act to suppress pro-Jefferson comment in the run-up to the presidential election of 1800, when Jefferson would oppose Adams. Its political cast was made transparent by the fact that it punished criticism of the president and Congress, but not of the vice president. The act itself provided that it would expire on March 3, 1801, the day before the next presidential inauguration. In the little more than two and one-half years of its existence, fourteen men were prosecuted under the act. Among them were the editors and proprietors of the leading Jeffersonian news-papers: the *Philadelphia Aurora*, the *Boston Independent Chronicle*, the *New York Argus*, the *Baltimore American*, and the *Richmond Examiner.* Most of the cases came to trial in the very year of the election, 1800. Adams's secretary of state, Timothy Pickering, encouraged prosecutions that would silence pro-Jefferson papers during the election year.

The law's stated requirement that a statement be "false" to be criminal was described by its sponsors as a liberalizing re-form of the common law of seditious libel, which did not allow the truth of criticisms as a defense. But in practice it was a distinction without a difference. Judges made those charged with violating the Sedition Act bear the burden of proving that their statements were true in all respects, and men were prosecuted for expressions of opinion, which could not be proved true.

The repressive nature of the law was made clear by the first prosecution. It was of a Republican member of Congress, Matthew Lyon of Vermont. He was charged for a letter to the editor he had written to the *Vermont Journal.* It said the pres-ident was engaged in "a continual grasp for power, in an un-bounded thirst for ridiculous pomp, foolish adulation and selfish avarice." It was political slanging, hardly to be judged true or false. But an indictment charged that Lyon's words were "scurrilous, feigned, false, scandalous, seditious and ma-licious." Supreme Court Justice William Paterson presided at Lyon's trial. (The justices then had to act also as trial judges, riding a judicial circuit.) He charged the jury that it had to de-cide whether Lyon could have written his letter "with any other intent than that of making odious or contemptible the president and government, and bringing them both into disrepute." Lyon was convicted and sentenced to four months in prison and a fine of $1,000.

Another Sedition Act prosecution that drew much attention was of a political pamphleteer, James T. Callender. As the campaign of 1800 got under way, he published a book that called President Adams a "hoary headed incendiary" and said the choice was "between Adams, war and beggary, and Jefferson, peace and competency." (Harry Croswell was prosecuted for seditious libel under New York law in 1803, as mentioned in Chapter 1, for saying that Jefferson had paid Callender to publish that attack on Adams.) Callender was convicted in a trial before Supreme Court Justice Samuel Chase, whom Republicans regarded as virulently pro-Federalist. (Chase was impeached by the House after Republicans won a majority there in 1800, but not convicted in the Senate.) The jurors in the Callender trial were all Federalists. Modern research has found that judges and federal marshals packed juries with Federalists in Sedition Act trials.

Prosecutions like those of Matthew Lyon and James Callender aroused wide protests—remarkably wide, considering the difficulty of communication at the time. Lyon's prison term was due to expire on February 9, 1799, but he was unable to pay the fine and had to stay in prison. But leading Republicans around the country contributed to a fund for him. Senator Stevens T. Mason of Virginia brought the money in gold to Vermont, and Lyon was released to a triumphal parade in his honor.

The Federalists' design to use the Sedition Act for political advantage badly miscarried. Jeffersonians denounced the prosecutions as attempts to take America back to the tyranny of George III; they published the transcript of Callender's trial as evidence of that intention. The law became a campaign issue, contributing to the defeat of Adams by Jefferson in 1800. In that election the Federalists also lost control of both houses of Congress, and the party began fading into oblivion.

It was a great political debate. From the viewpoint of the twenty-first century, what is surprising is that it *was* political rather than legal. Today, opponents of such a statute would rush to court to assert that it violated the First Amendment. The Sedition Act's constitutionality was never tested in the Supreme Court during its brief life. If it had been, the Court would almost certainly have upheld the law. Three of the six members of the Supreme Court in 1800, Justices Chase, Paterson, and Bushrod Washington, had presided at Sedition Act trials without intimating any constitutional doubts.

But the Constitution and the First Amendment were not overlooked in the debate. They were invoked by critics as reasons for Congress and the public to oppose the law. In fact, the political and public debate over the Sedition Act brought out, at that early stage in United States history, arguments about the freedom of speech and press that are still with us.

In the House debate, Federalists argued that a power to prevent seditious attacks in the press—though it was not one of the powers specifically given to the new federal government by the Constitution—was a necessary incident of any government. Representative John Allen of Connecticut told the House to look at newspapers in Philadelphia, where the government then sat. They showed, he said, that a "dangerous combination" existed to "overturn and ruin the government," urging people "to raise an *insurrection.*" There were indeed Philadelphia newspapers hostile to the Adams administration, but they urged that it be turned out not by insurrection but by the ballot box.

Federalists rejected the relevance of the First Amendment because, they said, its clause guaranteeing "the freedom of the press" disallowed only prior restraints—and the Sedition Act called for subsequent punishment. It was Blackstone's argument. In reply, Albert Gallatin of Pennsylvania (who became secretary of the treasury in Jefferson's administration) said it was "preposterous to say that to punish a certain act was not an abridgment of the liberty of doing that act." He called the Blackstone view "absurd" when applied to the free-speech clause of the First Amendment: How could a government apply prior restraints to men speaking, by sealing their mouths or cutting their tongues?

Representative John Nicholas, a Republican from Virginia, made an argument that anticipated free-speech theory two centuries later. Federalists defended the statute as liberal because it applied, at least in theory, only to false statements. Nicholas answered that any attempt to distinguish true from false was inconsistent with freedom. Any vigorous political criticism would be charged with falsehood, he said, and printers would be "afraid of publishing the truth as, though true, it might not always be in their power to establish the truth to the satisfaction of a court." In 1964, in the case of *New York Times v. Sullivan*, the Supreme Court said that "erroneous statement is inevitable in free debate, and . . . it must be protected if the freedoms of expression are to have the breathing space that they need to survive."

Nicholas made another important argument when the Republicans moved, unsuccessfully, in 1799 to repeal the Sedition Act. Its thinking, he said, came from Great Britain, which had a very different political structure. "The King is hereditary," he said, "and according to the theory of their government, can do no wrong. Public officers are his representatives, and derive some portion of his inviolability." But in America, "the officers of government are the servants of the people, are amenable to them, and liable to be turned out of office at periodical elections."

The most important voice heard in opposition to the Sedition Act was James Madison's. After its passage, he and Jefferson set out to arouse state legislatures against it. They acted in secret, for fear that they would be prosecuted themselves under the act—a leading drafter of the Constitution and the vice president of the United States! Jefferson wrote a resolution that the Kentucky legislature approved later in 1798. It made the argument of federalism—that the Constitution left to the states any power to adopt laws on the press. Madison wrote resolutions for the Virginia legislature making a classic argument that freedom of speech and of the press are the essential guardians of a republican political system.

The Virginia Resolutions, approved by the legislature in 1798, protested against "the palpable and alarming infractions

of the Constitution" in the Sedition Act. It exercised, the resolutions said,

> a power not delegated by the Constitution, but, on the con-
> trary, expressly and positively forbidden by one of the
> amendments thereto—a power which, more than any other,
> ought to produce universal alarm, because it is leveled
> against the right of freely examining public characters and
> measures, and of free communication among the people
> thereon, which has ever been justly deemed the only effec-
> tual guardian of every other right.

(John Adams had expressed virtually the same idea thirty-
three years earlier in his treatise "A Dissertation on the
Canon and Feudal Law." He wrote: "Liberty cannot be preserved without a general knowledge among the people, who
have a right . . . and a desire to know; but besides this, they
have a right, an indisputable, unalienable, indefeasible, divine
right to that most dreaded and envied kind of knowledge, I
mean of the characters and conduct of their rulers.")

Madison's phrase "the right of freely examining public
characters and measures" really expresses the premise of the
American political system: the Madisonian premise, we may
call it. It tells us why Americans should scent danger when a
government tries to stop a newspaper from disclosing the origins of an unsuccessful war, as the Nixon administration did
when the *New York Times* began publishing the Pentagon Papers on the Vietnam War in 1971, or accuses a newspaper of
endangering national security by disclosing secret and illegal

wiretapping without warrants, as the administration of George W. Bush did during the Iraq War in 2006.

Madison expounded his ideas further in a "Report on the Virginia Resolutions" that the legislature approved in January 1800. Under our Constitution, he said, "The people, not the government, possess the absolute sovereignty." That was "altogether different" from Britain—the point that Representative Nicholas had made: "Is it not natural and necessary, under such different circumstances, that a different degree of freedom in the use of the press should be contemplated?" In America, Madison said, "the press has exerted a freedom in canvassing the merits and measures of public men, of every description, which has not been confined to the strict limits of the Common Law. On this footing the freedom of the press has stood; on this foundation it yet stands."

There were dissenters in the Virginia House of Delegates, and they published a "minority address" in support of the Sedition Act—drafted by Henry Lee, a Revolutionary War hero known as Light Horse Harry Lee (and the father of Robert E. Lee). It posed in stark terms the choices that any society had to make then, and does now, about freedom of political expression. The minority argued:

To contend that there does not exist a power to punish writings coming within the description of this law would be to assert the inability of our nation to preserve its own peace, and to protect themselves from the attempts of wicked citizens who, incapable of quiet themselves, are incessantly employed in devising means to disturb the public repose. Government

is instituted and preserved for the general happiness and
safety; the people therefore are interested in its preservation,
and have a right to adopt measures for its security, as well
against secret plots as open hostility. But government cannot
be thus secured if, by falsehood and malicious slander, it is to
be deprived of the confidence and affection of the people.

That minority address was a fascinating expression of the
political premises that underlay the Sedition Act. It saw government as a sovereign that had to be protected from "wicked
citizens" rather than as a body chosen by sovereign citizens to
govern temporarily. And it saw danger in speech as uncon-
spiratorial as Matthew Lyon's mocking of John Adams.

When Jefferson became president in 1801, he quickly pardoned all the men who had been convicted for violating the
Sedition Act. He gave his reasons in an 1804 letter to Abigail
Adams. (Despite their bitter relations before the election of
1800, Jefferson had a long and friendly correspondence with
Abigail and, after a while, John Adams. They were close until
the two ex-presidents died—on the same day, July 4, 1826, the
fiftieth anniversary of the Declaration of Independence.) Jefferson wrote Mrs. Adams: "I discharged every person under
punishment or prosecution under the Sedition Law, because I
considered, and now consider, that law to be a nullity, as absolute and palpable as if Congress had ordered us to fall down
and worship a golden image; and that it was as much my duty
to arrest its execution in every stage, as it would have been to
have rescued from the fiery furnace those who should have
been cast into it for refusing to worship the image."

The Sedition Act inadvertently made a significant contribution to American freedom. It made numbers of Americans appreciate the importance of free speech and freedom of the press in a republic: the Madisonian premise. Whether or not the authors of the First Amendment intended to eliminate the crime of seditious libel, ten years after it was added to the Constitution the weight of American opinion was that such a crime was inconsistent with constitutional values.

But one feature of the Sedition Act did not disappear: the political use of fear to justify repression. Again and again in American history the public has been told that civil liberties must be sacrificed to protect the country from foreign threats. There have been repeated examples of what Richard Hofstadter called "the paranoid style in American politics." As in 1798, when the Federalists spoke of French terror to justify the Sedition Act, so in the twentieth century Congress passed many laws branding as infamous anyone who was suspected of a Communist taint; politicians from the 1920s through Richard Nixon and Joe McCarthy won votes by charging their opponents with being soft on communism. In the "war on terror" in the twenty-first century, President George W. Bush persuaded Congress to deprive alleged "enemy combatants" of legal rights in order, he said, to keep the country safe.

James Madison foresaw the problem. Two months before the Sedition Act was passed, in a letter to Vice President Jefferson, he wrote: "Perhaps it is a universal truth that the loss of liberty at home is to be charged to provisions against danger, real or pretended, from abroad."

3

"As All Life Is
an Experiment"

The First Amendment today is regularly and successfully invoked in lawsuits. The Supreme Court and other courts enforce its guarantees of free speech and freedom of the press. So it is astonishing to realize that the first time a Supreme Court opinion ever supported a claim of freedom under the amendment was in 1919—and that was a dissenting opinion. It was only 120 years after the Sedition Act that the speech and press clauses became a serious issue of law.

There were reasons for that long silence. The federal government had no laws restricting speech or publication from the end of the Sedition Act in 1801 until 1917. And the First Amendment, by its terms, applied only to federal laws, not state. ("*Congress* shall make no law . . . ") In 1833 the Supreme Court, in an opinion by Chief Justice Marshall, made clear that the entire Bill of Rights, the first ten amendments, covered only federal action.

The Fourteenth Amendment, added after the Civil War, provided that no state could "deprive any person of life, liberty, or property, without due process of law." The Supreme Court soon began to read that clause as guaranteeing individuals' property rights against state regulation, but at first it did not apply the clause to personal liberties of the kind protected by the first ten amendments, like freedom of speech.

When free-speech claims did reach the Supreme Court in the nineteenth century, it gave them the back of its hand, treating freedom of expression as an unimportant interest. The Court's approach was to allow repression of any speech that had a "bad tendency." That meant speech that might offend right-thinking people: a category so vague that it really offered no protection to speakers or writers. As late as 1907 this doctrine was used by a great Supreme Court justice, Oliver Wendell Holmes Jr., in a case called *Patterson v. Colorado*. Thomas M. Patterson, an editor, had been held in contempt of court for criticizing a judge. Under the old common-law rule, he was not allowed to argue that his criticism was true; Patterson argued that that denied him due process of law. Justice Holmes, following Blackstone, said "the main purpose" of the free speech guarantee was to prevent "previous restraints upon publication." The guarantee, he said, did "not prevent the subsequent punishment of such as may be deemed contrary to the public welfare." Even true statements could be punished if they did social harm, as criticism of a judge might in lowering respect for the administration of justice. That view echoed English seditious libel law. It gave no meaningful protection to speech or press, because just about anything might be "deemed contrary to the public welfare."

Justice John Marshall Harlan, dissenting, urged that the Fourteenth Amendment should be understood to have incorporated the guarantees of free speech and press in the First—and said that the judgment of contempt imposed on the editor violated those guarantees. Harlan's opinion was brief, three paragraphs, and without any discussion of the nature or scope of the freedom of speech and press. But it should be noted as a prescient call for applying those rights to state cases: a step that the Supreme Court did not take until 1925.

A dozen years later, Justice Holmes changed his mind—with profound consequences for American freedom. It is a remarkable story, still marked by a bit of mystery. The story starts with American entry into World War I, in 1917. The mood of the country turned jingoistic. Dissent from the war was not tolerated. German names were changed; sauerkraut became "liberty cabbage." In that atmosphere President Woodrow Wilson sought, and Congress passed, a sweeping Espionage Act. The act made it a crime to "cause or attempt to cause insubordination, disloyalty, mutiny, or refusal of duty in the military or naval forces" in wartime or to "willfully obstruct the recruiting or enlistment service." Hundreds of people were prosecuted under the act for merely speaking or writing critically. The most innocuous criticism of government or the war was found to violate the Espionage Act; judges told juries to convict if they found a defendant's words "disloyal."

In March 1919 three cases involving the Espionage Act were decided by the Supreme Court—all three unanimously, all three in opinions by Justice Holmes, all three upholding criminal convictions for violation of the act. At first glance there was little solace in the opinions for believers in freedom of speech.

In the first case, *Schenck v. United States*, the defendants had given leaflets denouncing conscription as slavery to men called up in the draft. Justice Holmes said, with what seemed reluctance, that "it may well be" that the First Amendment's guarantee of free speech "is not confined to previous restraints, . . . as intimated in *Patterson v. Colorado.*" But in exigent circumstances speech could be punished, he said, producing an analogy that has become famous but is not really a fair analogy to criticizing government policy: "The most stringent protection of free speech would not protect a man in falsely shouting fire in a theater and causing a panic."

Then Justice Holmes offered a formula for deciding when speech can be punished. "The question in every case," he said, "is whether the words used are used in such circumstances and are of such a nature as to create a clear and present danger that they will bring about the substantive evils that Congress has a right to prevent." Those Delphic words have been scrutinized by generations of scholars. Holmes said years later that the concept of "clear and present danger" came from the discussion of attempted crimes in his 1881 book, *The Common Law.* An attempt can be punished, he said then, if "its natural and probable effect" would in time have led to a crime. That approach did not seem protective of speech, and Holmes almost certainly did not intend it to be. It did not help the *Schenck* defendants—or those in the two other cases decided at that time, *Frohwerk v. United States* and *Debs v. United States.*

The *Debs* case made plain how far-reaching punishment for speech could be. The defendant was a well-known political figure: Eugene V. Debs, leader of the Socialist Party and five times its candidate for president. He was prosecuted for a speech he made in Canton, Ohio. It was mostly about socialism, but he began by telling the audience that he had just visited three men who were in jail nearby for aiding another man in failing to register for the draft. As Holmes put it in his opinion, Debs said the three "were paying the penalty for standing erect and for seeking to pave the way to better conditions for all mankind." Debs was convicted and sentenced to ten years in prison. (He was released after three years, having run for president in 1920 from a federal penitentiary.)

Holmes brushed off First Amendment arguments made for Debs, saying that his opinion in the *Schenck* case had disposed of them. He said there was evidence to "warrant the jury" in finding that Debs's opposition to the war and conscription "was so expressed that its natural and intended effect would be to obstruct recruiting." To appreciate how little weight Holmes gave to freedom of speech in the *Debs* case, think of the later American wars in Vietnam and Iraq. They were denounced in words far rougher than Debs's, but no one was prosecuted for mere speech. What Debs said in Canton did not actually harm recruiting efforts, but Holmes evidently felt that the clear and present danger test was met because the potential harm in wartime, however unlikely, was so great.

Just eight months later, in November 1919, the Supreme Court decided a fourth Espionage Act case, *Abrams v. United States.* Four radicals, refugees from the pogroms and tyranny of czarist Russia, protested President Wilson's decision to send American troops into Russia after the Bolshevik Revolution. They threw leaflets from the top of a building in New York's Lower East Side, urging a general strike in protest against Wilson's intervention. The four were charged under amendments to the Espionage Act, passed by Congress in 1918, which made it a crime to "utter, print, write or publish any disloyal, profane, scurrilous, or abusive language" about the Constitution, the armed forces, military uniforms, or the flag. The charge was that their leaflets, though they discussed the Russian intervention, were an attempt to hurt the war against Germany. All four were convicted. Three men were sentenced to twenty years in prison; Mollie Steimer, a twenty-year-old woman, to fifteen years.

The Supreme Court affirmed the convictions. But this time Justice Holmes dissented in an opinion joined by Justice Louis D. Brandeis. Holmes said he did not doubt the rightness of the three earlier Espionage Act decisions. The United States, he said, had the power to "punish speech that produces and is intended to produce a clear and imminent danger that it will bring about forthwith certain substantive evils." Holmes said he was merely restating his "clear and present danger" test, but he had added two crucial adjectives, "imminent" and "forthwith."

"Now nobody can suppose," Holmes wrote, "that the surreptitious publishing of a silly leaflet by an unknown man, without more, would present any immediate danger that its opinions would hinder the success of the government arms. . . . In this case sentences of twenty years imprisonment have been imposed for the publishing of two leaflets that I believe the defendants had as much right to publish as the Government has to publish the Constitution of the United States now vainly invoked by them." Holmes called the leaflets "poor and puny anonymities" and said that even if they could be found unlawful, only "the most nominal punishment" could be justified unless the defendants were really being punished for their radical views—views, he said, "that I believe to be the creed of ignorance and immaturity" but that "no one has a right even to consider in dealing with the charges before the Court."

It was a powerful dissent. Holmes made the case that savage sentences had been imposed for the publishing of words that only wartime zealotry could stretch into disruption of the war effort. But where had the opinion come from? Holmes always denied that his view in the *Abrams* case differed from what he had said in the three earlier Espionage Act decisions. But not only the outcome but the reasoning was quite different. By the standards of this opinion, Debs should not have been convicted for uttering a few sentences about meeting men who were imprisoned for advising on how to avoid draft registration.

How and why Holmes changed his mind, or at least changed his emphasis profoundly, cannot be said with certainty; that is where mystery remains. But there are clues. For one, the *Debs* decision had drawn widespread criticism from scholars and commentators who were usually admirers of Justice Holmes. We know that he read at least one of these criticisms, because he wrote a letter to the author—but did not mail it.

Another possible influence was Learned Hand, a federal trial judge in New York who later went on to the Court of Appeals and became probably the most respected judge in the country. Hand and Holmes met on a train in 1918. They evidently talked about freedom of speech, for they exchanged letters on the subject immediately afterward. Hand had written a striking opinion in favor of free speech in a case involving the radical magazine *The Masses*. The postmaster general had excluded it from the mails because of an issue that attacked the war and the draft. Judge Hand, ruling for the magazine in a suit against the exclusion order, *Masses Publishing Co. v. Patten* (1917), said speech that directly incited "violent resistance" could be punished—but not speech that merely criticized government policy, whether temperately or by invective. The distinction, he said, was "a hard bought acquisition in the fight for freedom." He added that a country with our constitutional commitment depended on "the free expression of opinion as the ultimate source of authority." That was a remarkable, telling point about political legitimacy. (Hand was reversed by the Court of Appeals, but his ideas survived.)

Hand wrote to Holmes, privately, after the *Debs* decision. Consistently with his *Masses* judgment, he said that speech should be punishable only when "directly an incitement" to illegality. He made a further point that was highly relevant in the wartime atmosphere. It was wrong to let juries decide whether words had a "tendency" to some bad result, he said, because the cases arise "when men are excited." Holmes replied, "I am afraid that I don't quite get your point." That seems most unlikely.

But the greatest influence on Holmes in this period was an article in the *Harvard Law Review* by Professor Zechariah Chafee Jr. of the Harvard Law School. Chafee was a scholar on freedom of speech, and he marshaled evidence from history to argue that the First Amendment gave broad protection to speech even in the agitated circumstances of wartime. He said the Framers of the amendment intended "to wipe out the common law of sedition and make further prosecutions for criticisms of the government, without any incitement to law-breaking, forever impossible in the United States."

Chafee might have been expected to attack the three decisions of March 1919 upholding Espionage Act convictions. To the contrary, he praised Holmes's "clear and present danger" formula, saying it would make "the punishment of words for their bad tendency impossible." He did say that the *Debs* jury should have been required to find a clear and present danger of illegal actions.

The Chafee article, entitled "Freedom of Speech in War Time," appeared in the *Harvard Law Review* issue of June 1919. It could not have been better timed. Holmes read it that summer, and years later he told Chafee in a letter that he had been "taught" by it about the historical roots of the First Amendment. But it would be a mistake to attribute Holmes's thinking entirely to this or that source. He was a phenomenal reader: He often read a book a day, and he read books in various languages.

When he came to write the *Abrams* dissent, Holmes relied on his own rhetorical power—which was extraordinary. He did not stop with the passage quoted above. He went on in words that forever changed American perceptions of freedom:

> Persecution for the expression of opinions seems to me perfectly logical. If you have no doubt of your premises or your power and want a certain result with all your heart, you naturally express your wishes in law and sweep away all opposition. . . .
>
> But when men have realized that time has upset many fighting faiths, they may come to believe even more than they believe the very foundations of their own conduct that the ultimate good desired is better reached by free trade in ideas—that the best test of truth is the power of the thought to get itself accepted in the competition of the market, and that truth is the only ground upon which their wishes safely can be carried out.
>
> That at any rate is the theory of our Constitution. It is an experiment, as all life is an experiment. . . . While that experiment is part of our system I think that we should be eternally vigilant against attempts to check the expression of opinions that we loathe and believe to be fraught with death, unless they so imminently threaten immediate interference with the lawful and pressing purposes of the law that an immediate check is required to save the country. . . .

Only the emergency that makes it immediately dangerous to leave the correction of evil counsels to time warrants making any exception to the sweeping command, "Congress shall make no law . . . abridging the freedom of speech." Of course I am speaking only of expressions of opinion and exhortations, which were all that were uttered here, but I regret that I cannot put into more impressive words my belief that in their conviction upon this indictment the defendants were deprived of their rights under the Constitution of the United States.

No other judge, then or since, could have written "It is an experiment, as all life is an experiment"—or "opinions that we loathe and believe to be fraught with death." Holmes was the closest we have had to a poet judge.

There was a remarkable episode on the way to Holmes's dissent in the *Abrams* case. It was unknown until Dean Acheson, the former secretary of state, told the story in 1965 in his memoir, *Morning and Noon*. Acheson was Justice Brandeis's law clerk in the 1920 Supreme Court term. His friend Stanley Morrison had clerked for Justice Holmes the year before, the *Abrams* year. Morrison told him that before the decision was announced, three other justices had called on Holmes, bringing Mrs. Holmes with them. Acheson wrote:

> They laid before him their request that in this case, which they thought affected the safety of the country, he should, like the old soldier he had once been, close ranks and forego individual predilections. Mrs. Holmes agreed. The tone of the

discussion was at all times friendly, even affectionate. The justice regretted that he could not do as they wished. They did not press. Thus, fortunately, survived a most moving statement of liberal faith in freedom of thought and speech.

Holmes had been a Union soldier in the Civil War, and had been gravely wounded three times. (When he died, his Union Army uniform was found hanging in his closet.) His colleagues and his wife appealed to his patriotism, but he would not yield. He dissented in his action as in his words—a perfect symbol of the point he was arguing, the legitimacy of dissent.

Justices Holmes and Brandeis were together in a stream of dissenting opinions in free speech cases over the next decade. They were a remarkable pair, alike in powerful intellects but differing sharply in other ways. Holmes was a Boston Brahmin, a lover of wine and women. Brandeis, the first Jewish member of the Supreme Court, was something of a Puritan who did not drink. After a brilliant record at the Harvard Law School, Brandeis made a fortune in private legal practice but devoted himself increasingly to legal work on behalf of the public. He was a social reformer; Holmes believed such efforts pointless. They had in common, though, a willingness to let governments experiment with such reforms as maximum hour laws, which led them to dissent when the Court held economic reform legislation unconstitutional. After Holmes's shift in 1919, they did not apply their deference to legislatures when free speech was at issue.

Claims for free speech regularly lost in the Court through the 1920s. There was just one notable victory. In *Gitlow v.*

New York (1925) Benjamin Gitlow challenged his conviction under New York law for a publication urging a "revolutionary dictatorship of the proletariat." The Court ruled against him, with a Holmes dissent joined by Brandeis. But the majority for the first time said that the Fourteenth Amendment applied the free-speech clause of the First to the states. Most free-speech cases in the Supreme Court from then on dealt with repression by state authorities.

Dissenting opinions are an appeal to "the brooding spirit of the law," Charles Evans Hughes said. That is, they call on future courts to rethink decisions. In fact, that rather seldom happens. But the dissents by Holmes and Brandeis between 1919 and 1929 did in time overturn the old, crabbed view of what the First Amendment protects. It was an extraordinary change, really a legal revolution. And it showed the power of words to change minds. Holmes and Brandeis had only two votes of nine. But their rhetoric was so powerful, so convincing, that it changed the attitude of the country and the Court.

Three opinions in that decade stand out. The first was Holmes's dissent in 1919 in the *Abrams* case. The second came in 1927 in the case of Anita Whitney, a member of a socially prominent family who helped to found the Communist Labor Party of California; she was convicted of membership in an organization advocating "criminal syndicalism," a term for radical groups, and sentenced to one to fourteen years in the San Quentin penitentiary. In *Whitney v. California* (1927), Brandeis wrote an opinion, joined by Holmes, that many regard as the greatest judicial statement of the case for freedom of speech. It said in part:

Those who won our independence . . . believed liberty to be the secret of happiness and courage to be the secret of liberty. They believed that freedom to think as you will and to speak as you think are means indispensable to the discovery and spread of political truth; that without free speech and assembly discussion would be futile; that with them, discussion affords ordinarily adequate protection against the dissemination of noxious doctrine; that the greatest menace to freedom is an inert people; that public discussion is a political duty; and that this should be a fundamental principle of the American government. They recognized the risks to which all human institutions are subject. But they knew that order cannot be secured merely through fear of punishment for its infraction; that it is hazardous to discourage thought, hope and imagination; that fear breeds repression; that repression breeds hate; that hate menaces stable government. . . . Believing in the power of reason as applied through public discussion, they eschewed silence coerced by law—the argument of force in its worst form. Recognizing the occasional tyrannies of governing majorities, they amended the Constitution so that free speech and assembly should be guaranteed.

Fear of serious injury alone cannot justify suppression of free speech and assembly. Men feared witches and burnt women. . . .

Brandeis's opinion did not then represent the law, but it helped Anita Whitney. A month after the Supreme Court turned down her appeal, the governor of California, C. C.

Young, pardoned her, quoting the Brandeis dissent at length in his pardon message.

(The fate of the four radicals who lost in the *Abrams* case was different. They were released from prison in 1921 on condition that they go to the Soviet Union. Mollie Steimer and Jacob Abrams were unhappy with the tyranny they encountered under Leninism and left for Mexico. Hyman Lachowsky and Samuel Lipman stayed in the USSR—and died at the hands, respectively, of Soviet and Nazi terror.)

The third great dissent of that decade was in the case of *United States v. Schwimmer*, decided by the Supreme Court in 1929. Rosika Schwimmer was a pacifist, an immigrant from Hungary who applied for citizenship. The rules at the time required her to swear that she would take up arms to defend the United States—which as a pacifist she refused to do. She was denied the right to become a citizen, and the Supreme Court upheld the denial. Justice Holmes, who was then eighty-eight years old, said her refusal to swear was irrelevant, "as she is a woman over fifty years of age, and would not be allowed to bear arms if she wanted to." He said he did not agree with her pacifism and did not think "that a philosophical view of the world would regard war as absurd." But he concluded his opinion as follows:

> Some of her answers might excite popular prejudice, but if there is any principle of the Constitution that more imperatively calls for attachment than any other it is the principle of free thought—not free thought for those who agree with us but freedom for the thought that we hate. I think that we

should adhere to that principle with regard to admission into, as well as to life within this country. And recurring to the opinion that bars this applicant's way, I would suggest that the Quakers have done their share to make the country what it is, that many citizens agree with the applicant's belief and that I had not supposed hitherto that we regretted our inability to expel them because they believe more than some of us in the teachings of the Sermon on the Mount.

I add a personal note on how I first came to read Justice Holmes's opinion in the *Schwimmer* case. Some time around 1960, when I was reporting on the Supreme Court for the *New York Times*, I was talking with Justice Felix Frankfurter in his chambers. Suddenly, to make a point, he rose and strode across the room to his shelves of *United States Reports*, the volumes of Supreme Court opinions. He pulled one off the shelf, opened it, and handed it to me. It was the Holmes dissent in *United States v. Schwimmer.* I read. When I came to the final paragraph, ending ". . . Sermon on the Mount," I felt the hair rise on the back of my neck.

4

Defining Freedom

A majority on the Supreme Court began enforcing the constitutional guarantee of freedom of speech in 1931, in the case of *Stromberg v. California*. A California law forbade the display of a red flag "as a sign, symbol or emblem of opposition to organized government." The Court held the statute unconstitutional: the first time it had ever done so in the name of the First Amendment. Chief Justice Charles Evans Hughes, who had joined the Court a year earlier, wrote the opinion for a 7-to-2 majority. "The maintenance of the opportunity for free public discussion to the end that government may be responsible to the will of the people and that changes may be obtained by lawful means," Hughes wrote, "is a fundamental principle of our constitutional system." The rhetoric had not the thrill of Holmes or Brandeis, but it operated from their premise: that free speech was a basic American value, that repression was not to be tolerated to prevent some dim and distant bad tendency.

Once the Court embarked on enforcing the First Amendment as law, it faced a new task: defining from case to case what the words of the amendment mean. That may sound simple. What could be more direct than the command, "Congress shall make no law . . . abridging the freedom of speech, or of the press"? But in fact, giving concrete meaning to those words was a daunting, and endless, job.

The language of the amendment sounds all-embracing, but does it really mean that the law cannot act against anything spoken or printed? Hardly. Blackmail is carried on by speech or writing, but the First Amendment does not protect the blackmailer—or the gangster who threatens violence if his demands are not met. The First Amendment is not a license to publish a copyrighted work without permission.

Conversely, the First Amendment has been interpreted to protect some actions that are not literally spoken or printed. That is true of the *Stromberg* case. Yetta Stromberg did not use words; she was prosecuted for carrying a red flag. The Supreme Court saw that as symbolic speech, the beginning of a long line of cases in which expressive acts have been protected. A notable example was the 1989 decision in *Texas v. Johnson*, reversing, on First Amendment grounds, a conviction for burning the American flag in a political demonstration.

How, then, is a judge to interpret the First Amendment? One approach would be to look at what James Madison, its drafter, and those who voted for it in 1791 thought they were doing. After all, they prohibited Congress from "abridging the freedom of speech. . . ." The word "the" can be read to mean what was understood at the time to be included in the concept of free speech.

The trouble with that approach, or one trouble, is that it is not at all clear what the Framers of the First Amendment had in mind. No definitions of freedom were offered in the congressional consideration, so far as we know, and it is impossible to get any useful guidance on the views of the many state legislators who voted to ratify the amendment.

The evident truth is that those who gave us the First Amendment did not provide a detailed code of how it was to be applied—and did not want to. They deliberately wrote a spacious amendment—a "sweeping command," as Justice Holmes put it in his *Abrams* dissent—and left it to later generations to apply its broad call for freedom to particular situations.

Holmes himself made one of the classic statements on the futility of looking to 1791 or 1787 for answers to constitutional questions. He wrote in 1920: "When we are dealing with words that also are a constituent act, like the Constitution of the United States, we must realize that they have called into life a being the development of which could not have been foreseen completely by the most gifted of its begetters. . . . The case before us must be considered in the light of our whole experience and not merely in that of what was said a hundred years ago."

Chief Justice Hughes also addressed the issue, in 1934: "If by the statement that what the Constitution meant at the time of its adoption it means today, it is intended to say that the great clauses of the Constitution must be confined to the interpretation which the Framers, with the condition and outlook of their time, would have placed upon them, the statement carries its own refutation."

Fifty years after Hughes wrote that, a legal movement arose that took the position he regarded as self-evidently wrong. Its supporters, including some judges and professors, became known as Originalists—because they advocated giving clauses of the Constitution their "original meaning." Their argument was that, in a sea of possible interpretations, the only course that kept judges from reading their own preferences into constitutional language was to look for the intention of the Framers. The most prominent Originalist was Justice Antonin Scalia of the Supreme Court. He and others ran into the difficulty, noted above, of finding an original intention when the authors or supporters of a clause in the Constitution had not expressed one, indeed had not even imagined the problem now at issue. Justice Scalia, a strong believer in freedom of expression, applied the First Amendment often without any reference to original intent. He joined, for example, in the decision finding unconstitutional the law against flag-burning.

Justice Hugo L. Black, whose long service on the Supreme Court (1937–1971) was marked by devotion to freedom of expression, sought in a different way to limit the interpretive discretion of judges. He read the First Amendment, he said, as "an absolute" that forbade any official restrictions on expression. But on occasion Justice Black found ways to uphold restrictions, saying for example that speech had occurred in an inappropriate place or was not really speech. When a young protester against the Vietnam War was prosecuted by California for wearing a jacket inscribed with the phrase "Fuck the Draft" in *Cohen v. California* (1971), the Supreme

Court found the protest protected by the First Amendment; but Justice Black joined a dissent that called it an "absurd and immature antic, . . . mainly conduct and not speech."

One important issue, in applying the amendment over many decades, was whether it gave any protection to false statements. The early cases were about beliefs and opinions, which cannot be judged true or false—"expressions of opinion and exhortations," as Holmes put it in his *Abrams* dissent. But what about statements of fact? If they include falsehoods, are they entitled to constitutional protection?

In 1925 the Minnesota legislature decided to close down scandal-mongering newspapers that often attacked legislators and other public officials. It passed a curiously named Public Nuisance Law that allowed the courts to enjoin—shut down—any "malicious, scandalous and defamatory newspapers." The statute allowed a newspaper to defend itself by showing that it had published the truth—but only if it had done so "with good motives and for justifiable ends." That condition effectively canceled the defense of truth, allowing judges to appraise the character of publishers.

A weekly paper called the *Saturday Press*, put out by Jay M. Near, became a target of the law in 1927. Near was a virulent anti-Semite. His paper regularly charged that Jewish gangsters, in league with officials, were corrupting government. After only nine issues, the *Saturday Press* was closed by court order. Near appealed to the Minnesota Supreme Court, which turned him down. "Our constitution," the court said, "was never intended to protect malice, scandal and defamation when untrue or published with bad motives or without justifiable ends. It is a shield for the honest, careful and conscientious press."

The established newspapers of Minnesota, no doubt thinking themselves honest, careful, and conscientious, took no interest in Jay Near's plight. But Robert Rutherford McCormick, the splenetic conservative publisher of the *Chicago Tribune*, recognized that leaving it to judges to decide who was a nice publisher would eviscerate freedom of the press; he decided to support Near. His lawyer, Weymouth Kirkland, took the case to the Supreme Court of the United States.

James E. Markham, deputy attorney general of Minnesota, who argued *Near v. Minnesota* for the state, may have hoped for help from Justice Brandeis because of Near's anti-Semitism. But from the bench Brandeis, who had obtained and read the nine published issues of the *Saturday Press*, told Markham that Near had tried to expose "combinations between criminals and public officials." We know, he added, "that just such criminal combinations exist to the shame of some of our cities." For a newspaper to expose them was bound to involve defamation, he said; if they got it wrong, they could be sued later for libel.

That was where the Supreme Court came out. By the narrowest of majorities, 5 to 4, the Court found the ban on the *Saturday Press* in violation of the First Amendment, as applied to the states by the Fourteenth. It was a turning point for freedom of the press.

Chief Justice Hughes, for the majority, found that the injunction against Near was a prior restraint of the kind rejected by Blackstone. He quoted Madison on the need for a free press. "The impairment of the fundamental security of life and property by criminal alliances and official neglect," he wrote, "emphasizes the primary need of a vigilant and courageous press, especially in great cities." Robert R. McCormick had those words inscribed in the lobby of his new building in Chicago, the Tribune Tower.

The four dissenters, in an opinion by Justice Pierce Butler, quoted from a treatise on the Constitution by an early, much-respected Supreme Court justice, Joseph Story. The First Amendment, Story said, meant only that "every man shall be at liberty to publish what is true, with good motives and for justifiable ends"—the very condition asserted by the Minnesota law. "Without such a limitation," Story added, the amendment "might become the scourge of the republic, . . . by rendering the most virtuous patriots odious through the terrors of the press, introducing despotism in its worst form." Contemporary critics of the press could not do better than his warnings against the press's "terrors" and "despotism."

I have taken my description of the *Near* case from a wonderful book by Fred Friendly, *Minnesota Rag*. Friendly was a CBS executive, a colleague of Edward R. Murrow, and later a vice president of the Ford Foundation. In writing the book he had an experience that is an illuminating coda to the case of *Near v. Minnesota*. At lunch one day in the Ford Foundation, Friendly spoke about his work on the book. A foundation trustee, Irving Shapiro, then the CEO of the DuPont Corporation, came over and said, to Friendly's astonishment, that he had known Jay Near. Shapiro's father owned a dry-cleaning store in Minneapolis. One day gangsters came in and demanded protection money. When Mr. Shapiro said no, they sprayed the clothes hanging in the store with acid. Irving, a young boy, watched from the back of the store. The established local papers did nothing with the story. But Mr. Near came in, wrote about the attack—and the gangsters were prosecuted. Fred Friendly tells the story.

Near v. Minnesota was and remains a bulwark of American press freedom. Because of that decision, it is very difficult to persuade a judge to issue a prior restraint on the press. It is a sharp contrast from the law in Britain, where courts routinely do such things as prohibit the publication of a book when someone asserts that he will be libeled in it.

Just five years after the *Near* decision the dissenting justices abandoned their opposition. Huey Long, the dictatorial populist governor of Louisiana, put through a newspaper tax to punish papers critical of him. The Supreme Court unanimously held it unconstitutional in *Grosjean v. American Press Co.* (1936). The opinion of the court, by Justice George Sutherland, one of the four conservative dissenters in 1931, cited the *Near* case. It rested on the informing function of the press, the point that Brandeis had made at the argument of the *Near* case and that Chief Justice Hughes had described in his opinion. The people, Sutherland wrote, are entitled to "full information in respect of the doings or misdoings of their government; informed public opinion is the most potent of all restraints upon misgovernment."

In his *Near* opinion Hughes did not rule out all prior restraints. No one would doubt, he said, that the government could prevent "publication of the sailing dates of transports or the number or location of troops." Forty years later, that language—the *Near* exception, it was called—became the crux of one of the greatest conflicts over freedom of the press, the Pentagon Papers case. In June 1971, the *New York Times* began publishing top-secret documents from a secret official history of the Vietnam War. The war was still on, and President Richard M. Nixon asserted that the stories threatened the national security. The courts temporarily stopped publication. Lawyers and judges debated whether what was in the papers amounted to Hughes's sailing dates of troopships.

In *New York Times v. United States*, a 6-to-3 majority of the Supreme Court, ruling just two weeks after the case began, held that the *Times* and other newspapers could resume publication of the Pentagon Papers. There were ten different opinions, offering diverse arguments. The most powerful, and no doubt the most lasting, came from Justice Black. It was his last opinion, before his illness and death that summer. Justice Black wrote:

The press was protected [in the First Amendment] so that it could bare the secrets of government and inform the people. Only a free and unrestrained press can effectively expose deception in government. And paramount among the responsibilities of a free press is the duty to prevent any part of the government from deceiving the people and sending them off to distant lands to die of foreign fevers and foreign shot and shell. In my view, far from deserving condemnation for their courageous reporting, the New York Times, the Washington Post and other newspapers should be commended for serving the purpose that the Founding Fathers saw so clearly. In revealing the workings of government that led to the Vietnam War, the newspapers nobly did precisely that which the Founders hoped and trusted they would do.

The *Near* decision freed the author of a damaging statement from the need to prove its truth before publication; with rare and extreme exceptions, judges must reject demands for prior restraints without examining the character of the statement. But what about a libel suit after publication? Could the target of an offensive newspaper story demand then that the author or publisher prove its truth? That question was resolved by the Supreme Court in 1964 in one of its most dramatic and far-reaching First Amendment decisions, *New York Times v. Sullivan.*

The case arose out of the civil rights movement in the American South. Its leader, Dr. Martin Luther King Jr., was convinced that the public in the North would reject racial segregation and discrimination if confronted with their cruelty. His strategy, based on the nonviolent approach of Mahatma Gandhi, was to demonstrate against racism and show Americans, most of whom knew little about its brutal reality, what it meant. The press—newspapers, magazines, broadcasting—had a crucial role in that strategy, bringing the reality home to national audiences.

On March 29, 1960, the *New York Times* published an advertisement by supporters of Dr. King. At that date, six years after the Supreme Court decision in *Brown v. Board of Education* holding segregation in schools unconstitutional, not only schools but state universities remained segregated by race throughout the Deep South. In a number of states, blacks were prevented from voting by threats and murderous violence.

The advertisement said that racist southern officials had used lawless tactics against the civil rights movement—for example arresting Dr. King seven times on trumped-up charges and mistreating demonstrators. The ad mentioned no names. It spoke of "Southern violators of the Constitution." But one official, L.B. Sullivan, a commissioner of the city of Montgomery, Alabama, sued the *Times* for libel. He claimed that he could be identified as one of the "violators" because he was in charge of the Montgomery police and the ad charged them with misconduct.

The atmosphere in the white South was so hostile that a *New York Times* lawyer who went down to the libel trial from New York was advised to stay in a motel 40 miles from Montgomery under an assumed name. (Justice Black, who was from Alabama, observed in a concurring opinion in the case that if white people in Montgomery had happened to see the ad and connect it with Commissioner Sullivan, his "political, social and financial prestige" had "likely been enhanced.")

The trial took place in a state court before a judge, Walter B. Jones, who so admired the Confederacy that on the anniversary of its founding he seated the jurors in his courtroom in Confederate military uniforms. Judge Jones ruled that the advertisement was libelous and left just two questions to the jury: Did the ad refer to Sullivan, and if so, what damages should he get? The jury awarded him all he asked, $500,000, at that point the largest libel award in Alabama history.

Under Alabama law, any publication that was challenged in a libel action was presumed to be false; the burden was on the publisher to prove it true. That burden of proof, as it is called, is a crucial factor, because proving truth can be difficult. It was the rule in libel cases in the common law, and it remains the rule in English law today—one reason why British newspapers so often give up and settle when they are sued for libel. At the time of the *Sullivan* case it was the law in a number of states, not just Alabama.

Another traditional rule in libel cases, followed in Alabama and elsewhere, was that damage was presumed. The person suing did not have to prove actual damage, say to his career, as he or she would have to prove in other civil damage cases, such as medical malpractice. It was enough in libel to show that the challenged publication was of a kind that would harm reputation.

A third libel rule was that the publisher's fault was presumed. In other damage cases the plaintiff had to show that the doctor, say, had not followed approved practice and hence was negligent. In the common law of libel, it did not matter whether the publisher had printed his statement negligently or with any other fault. Even if he did his best to get the truth, he paid if he could not prove it. Lawyers called these the "three galloping presumptions" of libel law.

The *New York Times* could not meet the demand that it prove the ad true in all material respects. It admitted that there were some misstatements in it: Dr. King had been arrested four times, not seven, for example; the dining hall of a black college was not padlocked, as the ad said. The advertisement was therefore libelous, as Judge Jones found, under Alabama law.

The $500,000 judgment against the *Times* was a large blow to the paper. It was barely profitable in 1960. Moreover, other Montgomery commissioners and the governor of Alabama, John Patterson, also sued over the advertisement, and one of the commissioners soon won $500,000 from a jury. The *Times* seemed likely to owe $3 million—enough to put it out of business, its general counsel, James Goodale, said later. But more important than the financial problems of the *New York Times* was the effect on the civil rights movement. The *Sullivan* lawsuit could discourage not only the *Times* but all national press institutions from covering the movement because of the legal risks. Indeed, the suit may have been planned with that idea in mind. The *Montgomery Advertiser*—edited by Grover C. Hall Jr., a friend of Commissioner Sullivan—headlined a story about the libel cases, "State Finds Formidable Legal Club to Swing at Out-of-State Press." So the suit threatened Dr. King's whole strategy of displaying racism to the country. In the most fundamental way, it threatened the informing purpose of the First Amendment.

The *Times* took the case to the Supreme Court. It looks now like an easy case to win: a huge, menacing libel judgment for a plaintiff not even named in the advertisement. But it was not easy at the time, not at all. Libel had always been considered outside the protection of the First Amendment. No libel judgment had ever been found to violate the guarantees of freedom of speech and press.

That was the challenge facing the *Times*'s lawyer, Professor Herbert Wechsler of the Columbia Law School. He would have to ask the justices to do what courts are extremely reluctant to do: reverse a long-unchanged course of legal history. Wechsler decided to meet that history with another page of history: the record of the Sedition Act of 1798. He argued that the libel law of Alabama, as applied in this case, punished criticism of public officials just as the Sedition Act had done. And he said the Sedition Act, though never tested in the Supreme Court, had in effect been found unconstitutional when the voters rejected President Adams in 1800 and installed Thomas Jefferson, the act's critic, in his place.

Wechsler argued that there could be no test of truth for criticism of public officials. To allow libel judgments for any misstatement, he said, would discourage the press and individual citizens from voicing criticism lest they make a mistake. He told the Court: "This is not a time—there never is a time—when it would serve the values enshrined in the Constitution to force the press to curtail its attention to the tensest issues that confront the country."

At the oral argument of the case, Justice William J. Brennan Jr. asked Wechsler whether there were "any limits whatever" to the First Amendment's protection for criticism of officials. That is, was he proposing an absolute privilege for such criticism? Wechsler said he was. "If I take my instruction from James Madison," he said, "I can see no toying with limits." Justice Potter Stewart asked whether he would make the same argument if a newspaper accused an official of taking a bribe. "Certainly," Wechsler replied. "Of course, in the historic period in which Madison was writing, charges of bribery were common, and it was this type of press freedom that he saw in the First Amendment."

Justice Brennan delivered the opinion of the Court on March 9, 1964. It was a decisive victory for the *New York Times*, and a sweeping assertion of the values of free speech and freedom of the press. Quoting from Madison, Hand, and Brandeis, Justice Brennan adopted their views as the law of the Constitution. He said: "Thus we consider this case against the background of a profound national commitment to the principle that debate on public issues should be uninhibited, robust and wide-open, and that it may well include vehement, caustic, and sometimes unpleasantly sharp attacks on government and public officials."

Justice Brennan put the Sedition Act of 1798 at the heart of his analysis. The controversy over it, he said, "first crystallized a national awareness of the central meaning of the First Amendment"—the right to criticize what Madison called "public characters and measures." "Although the Sedition Act was never tested in this Court," Brennan said, "the attack upon its validity has carried the day in the court of history." With that, the Sedition Act was found unconstitutional 163 years after it expired.

Letting libel defendants escape damages by proving the truth of their criticism was not enough, Justice Brennan said: "Would-be critics of official conduct may be deterred from voicing their criticism, even though it is believed to be true and even though it is in fact true, because of doubt whether it can be proved in court or fear of the expense of having to do so." It was the same point made by Representative John Nicholas in the House debate on the Sedition Act in 1798.

But Justice Brennan did not go all the way with Madison and Wechsler. He did not say that the First Amendment required an absolute privilege for criticism of officials. Instead, he said that officials could not win libel damages from their critics unless they proved that a false, damaging statement had been made with knowledge of its falsity—a deliberate lie—or in "reckless disregard" of its truth or falsity. Later cases explained that "reckless disregard" meant the author or publisher was aware of the statement's probable falsity.

Six members of the Supreme Court joined in that resolution of *New York Times v. Sullivan*. Three—Justices Black, William O. Douglas, and Arthur Goldberg—said in concurring opinions that they would have gone farther and disallowed all libel actions by officials over criticism of their official conduct. Commentators have wondered why Justice Brennan did not agree with them. The *Sullivan* case was decided just after Senator Joseph McCarthy's demagogic career of denouncing as Communists or disloyal such persons as General George C. Marshall, a revered former secretary of state. Justice Brennan never spoke to the McCarthy problem as such, but in a lecture the year after the *Sullivan* decision he said:

At the time the First Amendment was adopted, as today, there were those unscrupulous enough and skillful enough to use the deliberate or reckless falsehood as an effective political tool. . . . That speech is used as a tool for political ends does not automatically bring it under the protective mantle of the Constitution. For the use of the known lie as a tool is at once at odds with the premises of democratic government and with the orderly manner in which economic, social or political change is to be effected.

New York Times v. Sullivan revolutionized the law of libel in the United States. What had always been a matter of state law became, in most cases, a subject that turned on federal constitutional law. The old common-law doctrine putting the burden on libel defendants to prove truth was reversed; decisions following the *Sullivan* case made clear that the plaintiff had to prove falsity in order to win—and had to prove fault on the part of the author or publisher, not just an innocent mistake.

The law of other countries was affected, too. Over the years since 1964, a number of courts abroad have adjusted their law of libel to give the authors of criticism more protection. Even the House of Lords, Britain's highest court, did so. But no other country went as far as the rule laid down by Justice Brennan.

The immediate consequence of the decision in this country was to open the way for intense coverage of the racial struggle in the South by a press freed from the threat of endless libel actions. Just as Dr. King had hoped, the violence directed at civil rights supporters made the brutal nature of racism clear to many in the North. There, on television, were grown men and women screaming obscenities at little black children trying to go to desegregated schools. Professor Alexander M. Bickel of the Yale Law School said, "The moral bankruptcy, the shame of the thing, was evident."

Public outrage put pressure on Congress to act, and it did. In 1964 it outlawed discrimination in public accommodations, schools, and jobs. In 1965 it passed the Voting Rights Act, which finally enabled black Americans to vote in the Deep South. The politics of the region was transformed, with blacks elected to many offices and southern Democrats moving en masse to the Republican Party. The First Amendment had worked exactly as Madison had hoped it would. Freedom of speech, and of the press, had empowered citizens in a democracy.

The effects of the *Sullivan* case were not limited to the immediate racial context. Over the years it emboldened the American press, encouraging it to challenge official truth instead of acting as a mere stenographer. Within a decade this new spirit of journalism produced two of the press's great modern achievements: penetrating coverage of the Vietnam War and Watergate. Young reporters on the ground in Vietnam found that the American war was not going well, and said so. Officials all the way up to presidents John F. Kennedy and Lyndon B. Johnson put heavy pressure on editors and publishers to curb their reporters, but they did not give way. The new spirit was symbolized by the decision of the *New York Times* to publish the Pentagon Papers in 1971. The next year, Bob Woodward and Carl Bernstein of the *Washington Post* began their epic exploration of the official crimes of Watergate. Officials threatened the publisher of the *Post*, Katharine Graham, with loss of the company's television channels; but she held fast. In 1974, after investigations provoked by the press, President Nixon was forced to resign.

In later cases the Supreme Court extended the *Sullivan* decision so that not only officials but "public figures" had to prove deliberate or reckless falsification to win damages for libel. It defined "public figures" to include people who are universally famous, like movie stars, or who thrust themselves into "the vortex of controversy" on some public issue—for example, a citizen who plays a significant part in a local zoning dispute. The press was pleased that more libel plaintiffs had to bear the heavy burden, but I was and remain unpersuaded. If a supermarket tabloid prints a sensational story about a movie actress, why should she have to meet the same test as a politician if she sues for libel? What does she have to do with what the *Sullivan* decision called "the central meaning of the First Amendment," the right to criticize government officials?

The *Sullivan* decision has been roundly criticized by some politicians who say it makes their life more difficult. It undoubtedly does. The decision has probably played a part in the vulgarization of the public dialogue in recent years—which affects all of us. Professor Vincent Blasi, a First Amendment scholar at Columbia University and the University of Virginia, put it this way: "Today's talk radio, wide open and factually casual, is the result of *Sullivan*." You can say practically anything about a public person without fear of having to pay damages.

The cacophony of talk radio and the bloggers can certainly be depressing. But it is very much like what existed in Madison's day, when newspapers were aggressively partisan and often reckless. After he had been president for six years, Jefferson wrote a friend: "Nothing can now be believed which is seen in a newspaper. Truth itself becomes suspicious by being put into that polluted vehicle."

Whatever the disagreements about the impact of *New York Times v. Sullivan*, one thing is clear. The decision finally put an end to the idea of seditious libel in this country. That is no small thing. In the twenty-first century many countries still prosecute people for saying things that lower the prestige of political leaders. A Turkish citizen who visited the home of modern Turkey's founder, Kemal Ataturk, wrote in the guest book an uncomplimentary comparison with the current prime minister—and then was punished with a hefty fine. Between 1995 and 2005, citizens of Indonesia, Malaysia, Swaziland, and Pakistan were prosecuted on charges of seditious libel or its equivalent for comments they had made about public officials or institutions. A law added to Russia's criminal code in 2006 made it a crime, punishable by up to three years in prison, to engage in "public slander directed toward figures fulfilling the state duties of the Russian Federation."

For many years the great American advocate of uninhibited political speech was Alexander Meiklejohn. He believed that the concept of seditious libel was inconsistent with the role of the citizen in a democracy. He was ninety-two years old when the *Sullivan* case was decided. When someone asked him what he thought about it, he replied, "It is an occasion for dancing in the streets."

5

Freedom and Privacy

The long struggle to give meaning to the First Amendment established that freedom of speech and of the press is a fundamental value in American society. But is it a paramount value, overriding others when they conflict with it? The question arises again and again, in the courts and in everyday life. All kinds of interests are involved: the right to a fair trial without inflammatory press coverage, the protection of racial or religious groups from hateful speech, the safeguarding of national security. Nowhere is the conflict likely to be more personal or more painful than on issues of privacy.

A child is paraded as a genius by a domineering father. Grown up, he rebels and retreats into hermit-like anonymity. But a magazine writer finds him and writes a mocking exposure. Should he be able to win damages from the magazine for destruction of his privacy?

That is the case, the tormenting case, of William James Sidis. Born in 1898, he was mentally force-fed by his father, Boris, a psychologist. William was reading the *New York Times* by the age

of eighteen months. So said his father, who trained him re-
lentlessly and issued bulletins on his accomplishments to the
press. William entered Harvard at age eleven, and the *Times*
described him as the "wonderfully successful result of a scientific forcing experiment."

As might have been predicted, Sidis rebelled against the life
of fame, seeking obscurity. He escaped press attention for
years—until, in 1937, *The New Yorker* published a piece about
him by Jared L. Manley. Under the headline "Where Are
They Now?" was the subhead "April Fool," a play on the fact
that Sidis was born on April 1. The article treated him with
contempt, noting his "curious laugh," his interest in the lore
of the Okamakamesset Indians, his collection of streetcar
transfers. (Sidis had actually published, anonymously, a book
called *Notes on the Collection of Transfers*; a biographer, Amy
Wallace, called it "arguably the most boring book ever written.") Manley's article described Sidis as living a lonely life in
"a hall bedroom in Boston's shabby South End."

Sidis sued for violation of his privacy. The case, *Sidis v. F-R
Publishing Corporation*, was decided in 1940 by the United
States Court of Appeals for the Second Circuit. The opinion
was by a particularly thoughtful judge, Charles Clark, a former
dean of the Yale Law School. Judge Clark expressed sympathy
for Sidis. He described the Manley article as "merciless," a
"ruthless exposure of a once public character" who had gone to
"pitiable lengths . . . to avoid public scrutiny" in his "passion for
privacy." The judge said there was no reason to doubt Sidis's
claims that the article had held him up to "public scorn, ridicule
and contempt," causing him "grievous mental anguish."

But Judge Clark rejected Sidis's legal claim. The court would not, he said, "afford to all the intimate details of private life an absolute immunity from the prying of the press." It would, rather, permit "limited scrutiny of the 'private' life of any person who has achieved, or has had thrust upon him, the questionable and indefinable status of a 'public figure.'" Sidis had not challenged the truth of the painful descriptions in the *New Yorker* piece, and Judge Clark said they must be allowed unless the revelations were "so intimate and so unwarranted in view of the victim's position as to outrage the community's notions of decency." In this instance, he concluded, the public had a legitimate interest in learning how the onetime boy genius had turned out.

"Thrust upon him," that phrase of Judge Clark's, is what makes the outcome of the case seem so cruel. Sidis was subject to public mocking for the rest of his life because of the fame his father had forced upon him. That was the balance Judge Clark struck between the freedom of journalism and the right to privacy. Might it have made a difference if the judge had known more about the journalism in this case?

In her book *Secrets*, Sissela Bok told us some surprising things about the *New Yorker* article on William Sidis. Its supposed author, Jared L. Manley, did not exist; it was a pseudonym for James Thurber, one of *The New Yorker*'s most esteemed writers. And apparently Thurber never met Sidis. The article said a woman, unnamed, had "recently succeeded in interviewing him." One wonders whether she disclosed that she was acting as an agent for Thurber, or posed as friendly to the lonely Sidis so she would be invited to visit him in the shabby South End and inspect his collection of street-car transfers. When Sidis's lawsuit went to court, Thurber explained that he wanted to "help curb the great American thrusting of talented children into the glare of fame and notoriety" by showing how the children suffered later. But Sissela Bok observed drily that such a purpose was not evident in Thurber's article, "the less so as its author did more than anyone else to renew the glare of notoriety for Sidis. What comes across, rather, is a distant and amused contempt for those judged to be doing less than they might, and living boring lives in one-room apartments."

Four years after the Second Circuit decision, Sidis, unemployed and destitute, died of a cerebral hemorrhage. He was forty-six.

There is an aspect of the Sidis case that must seem puzzling today: Judge Clark's opinion does not mention the First Amendment. That is because privacy, like libel, was then considered to be outside the scope of the amendment—a view that did not change until the *Sullivan* decision in 1964. But Judge Clark dealt with the case exactly as if the First Amendment were in it. He balanced Sidis's interest in privacy against the society's interest in freedom of comment. He decided the latter had greater weight because of the free-spoken society we are. Once someone becomes a public figure, however unwillingly, he or she is forever fair game for the press.

The interest of privacy was first authoritatively weighed against the First Amendment's guarantee of free expression by the Supreme Court in 1967, in the case of *Time, Inc. v.*

Hill. It is a remarkable case in several ways: the closeness of the competing interests, the surprising course of decision inside the Court, and the tragic nature of the denouement. James Hill, his wife, and five children lived in a suburb of Philadelphia. In 1952 three escaped convicts took over their home, keeping the Hills hostage but treating them respectfully. After the convicts left, they were caught. The press covered the story intensely, to the distress especially of Mrs. Hill. To escape publicity, the family moved to Connecticut and sought obscurity.

Two years later a play called *The Desperate Hours* opened on Broadway. It was about a family held hostage in its home by escaped convicts. Unlike the convicts who came to the Hills' home, the convicts in the play carried out a reign of terror: brutality, sexual threats, and general menace. The play was set in Indianapolis. But *Life* magazine, doing a feature on the opening, photographed the actors in the former home of the Hills near Philadelphia and described the play, with all its terror, as a reenactment of what had happened to the Hills. The *Life* story was devastating to the Hill family. Mrs. Hill suffered a psychiatric breakdown. Mr. Hill said he could not understand how *Life* could publish such a piece without at least telephoning him to check the facts. "It was just like we didn't exist," he said, "like we were dirt."

Mr. Hill sued Time, Inc., the publisher of *Life*, for violation of the New York privacy law. By associating his family with horrors that it had not in fact experienced, he said, the article showed the family in a false light. (Privacy law embraces four different concepts. One is called "false light privacy," which describes cases in which there are errors but no damage to reputation, as there is in libel. Other branches of privacy will be described later in this chapter.)

In the New York courts, Mr. Hill won damages of $30,000. But Time took the case on to the Supreme Court. There Mr. Hill was represented by Richard M. Nixon, who practiced law in New York in the years before his successful campaign for president in 1968. The case was argued on April 27, 1966; the justices thought Nixon performed well.

What happened then inside the Court was a secret until the appearance in 1985 of a book by Professor Bernard Schwartz, *The Unpublished Opinions of the Warren Court.* His account, taken from the papers of retired justices, has not been challenged. In their next conference after the argument, the justices voted 6 to 3 to uphold Mr. Hill's modest judgment. Chief Justice Earl Warren assigned the opinion to Justice Abe Fortas. His draft, which the Schwartz book reproduces, began with a stinging attack on *Life*'s handling of the story—and sarcastic comments on the behavior of some journalists:

> Needless, heedless, wanton and deliberate injury of the sort inflicted by *Life*'s picture story is not an essential instrument of responsible journalism. Magazine writers and editors are not, by reason of their high office, relieved of the common obligation to avoid inflicting wanton and unnecessary injury. The prerogatives of the press—essential to our liberty—do not preclude reasonable care and avoidance of casual infliction of injury. . . . They do not confer a license for pointless assault.

The Fortas draft also included an eloquent comment on the meaning of privacy and its place in a civilized society:

> It is of constitutional stature. . . . It is not only the right to be secure in one's person, house, papers and effects, except as permitted by law; it embraces the right to be free from coercion, however subtle, to incriminate oneself; it is different from, but akin to the right to select and freely to practice one's religion and the right to freedom of speech; it is more than the specific right to be secure against the Peeping Tom or the intrusion of electronic espionage devices and wiretapping. All of these are aspects of the right to privacy; but the right of privacy reaches beyond any of its specifics. It is, simply stated, the right to be let alone; to live one's life as one chooses, free from assault, intrusion or invasion except as they can be justified by the clear needs of community living under a government of law.

But Justice Fortas's words were never published by the Supreme Court. In the weeks after argument, members of the Court began to rethink their views. The justices ordered the case argued again the following fall. And then a new majority decided against Mr. Hill's privacy claim.

Before the reargument Justice Black, the Court's most passionate advocate of freedom of expression, sent a memorandum to his colleagues. It is printed in the Schwartz book. "After mature reflection," he wrote, "I am unable to recall any prior case in this Court that offers a greater threat to freedom of speech and press than this one does." His point was that the press, imperfect as it inevitably is, would be forced into self-censorship if it were subject to damages for mistakes that did not damage anyone's standing in the community—did not, that is, rise to the level of libel.

The decision came down in January 1967. A 5-to-4 majority set aside Mr. Hill's judgment in an opinion by Justice Brennan. He had written the landmark libel opinion three years earlier in *New York Times v. Sullivan*, holding that public officials could not recover damages for false and damaging reports unless the falsities were deliberate or reckless. Now Justice Brennan applied the same formula to the privacy claim of James Hill. *Life's* falsifying of the Hill family's story had not been proved knowing or reckless, he said, so *Life* was entitled to a new trial at which a jury would decide that question. But the *Sullivan* case had turned on what Justice Brennan called "the central meaning of the First Amendment," the right to criticize the government. How did that apply to speech about private citizens like the Hills? Justice Brennan gave this explanation:

> The guarantees for speech and press are not the preserve of political expression or comment upon public affairs, essential as those are to healthy government. One need only pick up any newspaper or magazine to comprehend the vast range of published matter which exposes persons to public view, both private citizens and public officials. Exposure of the self to others in varying degrees is a concomitant of life in a civilized community. The risk of this exposure is an essential incident of life in a society which places a primary value on freedom of speech and press.

That passage in Justice Brennan's opinion amounts to a rejection of privacy as an important value. The most obscure American, it says, one who wants urgently to avoid the public gaze, must accept "exposure of the self to others." That is the price of "life in a civilized community." I am a great admirer of Justice Brennan, but I disagree with his conception of a "civilized community."

Justice Fortas dissented, in an opinion that lacked the angry rhetoric of his draft. (His overheated tone there may have helped change justices' minds.) His opinion was joined by Chief Justice Warren and Justice Tom C. Clark. Justice John Marshall Harlan, grandson and namesake of the first Justice Harlan, wrote a separate dissenting opinion, making the vote 5 to 4 against the Hills. I find the Harlan opinion persuasive.

The Hill case, Justice Harlan said, did not involve an official or public figure, someone who could command an audience. If Mr. Hill protested the *Life* story, who would publish his comments? So the "marketplace" of free speech in which Justice Holmes said ideas must compete did not work. Justice Harlan said that raised the danger of "unchallengeable untruth." Accordingly, he would have required Mr. Hill to prove merely that *Life's* editors had been negligent in making their mistakes, rather than what is harder to prove, that their falsification was deliberate or reckless.

When Schwartz's book was published and the internal course of decision in *Time, Inc. v. Hill* became known, Richard Nixon—by then a resigned president—asked his former White House counsel, Leonard Garment, to look into it. Garment had worked on the Hill case as Nixon's law partner.

After reading the Schwartz account, Garment wrote an article for *The New Yorker*. He described Nixon's meticulous preparation for the two arguments of the case in the Supreme Court. He also described telephoning Nixon with the news that the Court had decided against him. Nixon said: "I always knew I wouldn't be permitted to win a big appeal against the press."

Garment noted a statement in Justice Harlan's opinion that unwanted publicity carried a "severe risk of irremediable harm . . . [to] individuals exposed to it and powerless to protect themselves against it." Garment said there had been testimony at the trial in New York that the *Life* article had caused "lasting emotional injury" to Mrs. Hill. Then Garment wrote: "Two eminent psychiatrists had explained the causal dynamics of the trauma inflicted on her. Both said she had come through the original hostage incident well but had fallen apart when the *Life* article brought back her memories transformed into her worst nightmares and presented them to the world as reality. Both said she was and would for an indefinite time remain a psychological tinderbox. In August, 1971, Mrs. Hill took her life."

The legal debate about privacy traces back to an extraordinary law review article: "The Right to Privacy," by Louis D. Brandeis and Samuel D. Warren, published in 1890 in the *Harvard Law Review*. It was extraordinary because it had more effect on the law than anything else ever written for a law review. In its wake most states have adopted rules of law to protect privacy by either legislation or judicial decisions.

The Brandeis-Warren article spoke of "the right to be let alone." Thirty-eight years later, Brandeis, a man of lasting convictions, used that phrase again in dissenting from a Supreme Court decision that said wiretapping was not a search subject to the restraints of the Fourth Amendment to the Constitution, which regulates searches and seizures by government agents. In *Olmstead v. United States* (1928) Justice Brandeis wrote:

> The makers of our Constitution . . . recognized the signifi-cance of man's spiritual nature, his feelings and his intellect. They knew that only a part of the pain, pleasure and satis-factions of life are to be found in material things. They sought to protect Americans in their beliefs, their thoughts, their emotions and their sensations. They conferred, as against the government, the right to be let alone—the most comprehensive of rights and the right most valued by civi-lized men.

The wiretapping decision from which Brandeis dissented was overruled by the Supreme Court in 1967, when taps were made subject to the Fourth Amendment. "The right to be let alone" has become a familiar phrase in law and life. (Justice Fortas used it, without attribution, in the tribute to privacy in his draft opinion in *Time, Inc. v. Hill.*) But the Brandeis-Warren law review article arose not from any general assault on pri-vacy but from a particular fact: Pictures of Warren's wife had been used without her permission.

Using someone's likeness without permission has devel-oped as one of the four branches of privacy law. A second is false light privacy, exemplified by the *Hill* case: putting someone in a false light by, for example, fictionalizing a story about him or her. (A colorful biography of a baseball pitcher invents a childhood scene in which his mother says, "Lefty, why do you keep throwing a ball at that chicken?") The third branch of privacy law, known as intrusion, is invasion of one's personal space by means, for example, of an eavesdropping device. The fourth is publication of truthful but embarrassing private facts.

The first of these, known as appropriation, has produced some colorful cases involving "look-alikes": people who look like famous individuals and masquerade as them. Woody Allen successfully sued to keep companies from using Phil Boroff, who looked like him, in advertising. Bette Midler was awarded $400,000 in damages by a jury from an advertising agency that used a sound-alike mimicking her famous voice.

Jacqueline Kennedy Onassis sued, and won, to stop a model who looked like her, Barbara Reynolds, from seeming to be her in advertisements. In her case, unlike others, she was not complaining of unfair commercial competition; she wanted the right not to have her face appear commercially. Reynolds claimed that her impersonation was constitutionally protected as art. Justice Edward J. Greenfield of the New York Supreme Court disagreed. "To paint a portrait of Jacqueline Kennedy Onassis is art," he said. "To look like Jacqueline Kennedy Onassis is not."

The third branch of privacy law, intrusion, was fascinatingly explored in a California case, *Shulman v. Group W Productions*, decided by the state Supreme Court in 1998. Like the cases of William Sidis and James Hill, the *Shulman* case saw the interest of free expression in conflict with poignant claims of privacy. Ruth Shulman was driving on a California highway when her car was hit by another and rolled down an embankment. She was gravely injured, ending up as a paraplegic. A rescue helicopter came to the scene of the accident and flew Shulman to a hospital. Without her knowledge, a member of the rescue party, a nurse, was wearing a microphone and recorded her conversation with Shulman at the scene and in the helicopter; someone else filmed her with a video camera. A program made from these recordings appeared on television, and Shulman sued for invasion of her privacy.

The California Supreme Court decided that Shulman could maintain her suit. Justice Kathryn M. Werdegar, rejecting First Amendment objections, said that government may not dictate what the news media "should publish and broadcast, but neither may the media play tyrant to the people by unlawfully spying on them in the name of news-gathering." She found that Shulman may reasonably have expected that her conversations with the nurse at the accident scene and in the helicopter were in a zone of privacy. It was up to a jury, she said, to decide whether the defendant broadcasters had invaded that zone, and whether such an invasion was "highly offensive to a reasonable person." That was in effect a narrowly defined exception to the broadcasters' First Amendment right to do a story on a newsworthy event. Two justices, dissenting, would have thrown out the lawsuit. But Justice Werdegar was surely in the spirit of Brandeis when she wrote:

A jury could reasonably believe that fundamental respect for human dignity requires the patients' anxious journey to be taken only with those whose care is only for them and out of the sight of prying eyes. . . . A reasonable jury could find that defendants, in placing a microphone on an emergency treatment nurse and recording her conversation with a distressed, disoriented and severely injured patient, without her consent, acted with highly offensive disregard for the patient's personal privacy.

The broadcasters settled the case, paying Shulman an unstated amount in damages. They must have guessed what jurors would think of their behavior.

The fourth branch of privacy law, publication of truthful but embarrassing facts, has produced some notable examples of conflict between the claims of privacy and freedom to publish. President Gerald R. Ford left the St. Francis Hotel in San Francisco on September 22, 1975, when a woman waiting there, Sara Jane Moore, raised a gun and pointed it at him. A former Marine in the crowd, Oliver S. Sipple, leapt forward and struck her arm. The shot missed the president; Sipple may have saved his life. Newspapers across the country described his daring. Two days later a well-known columnist in the *San Francisco Chronicle*, Herb Caen, wrote that Sipple was gay and was a hero in the city's gay community. Others copied the story, and across the country Sipple was identified as gay. He sued for violation of his privacy, arguing that he was indeed homosexual but was entitled to damages for disclosure of a fact that would embarrass him in some circles. The California courts ruled against him without resolving the conflict between his privacy and the press's freedom. They said his sexual orientation was known to many before the Caen column and hence was not really "private."

For decades the California courts were unusually hospitable to damage claims for publications that were truthful but embarrassing. The case of *Melvin v. Reid*, decided in 1931, involved a former prostitute who had been accused of murder but acquitted. In the years following, she had reformed, married, and become a respected member of the town where she lived. Then a movie called *The Red Kimono* was made about her life. It had an adverse effect on her social position, and she sued for violation of her privacy. She won the case. As late as 1971 the California Supreme Court followed that precedent, holding that even though a scandalous event was publicized at the time, a later story reminding readers of it could be a violation of privacy.

That view was in direct conflict with Judge Clark's decision in the *Sidis* case that once someone is a subject of public attention, he or she cannot escape that condition. More recently, the more generous interpretations of the First Amendment by the Supreme Court make it clear that the press may call attention truthfully to old facts, however embarrassing. In her opinion in the *Shulman* case, Justice Werdegar indicated that the California Supreme Court would no longer adhere to the precedent of the Red Kimono case. The American legal culture as it is today would not accept a prohibition on publication of facts already public. And search engines on the Internet have made just about everyone's past available to the public at a click. Once known, no fact of private life can be buried. But that still leaves open the question whether a prurient reporter or tabloid can be held liable for fresh invasions of privacy.

The press has urged the Supreme Court to hold that it may always publish the truth, no matter how much it may trouble someone. The Court has repeatedly refused to decide that large issue, instead resolving a series of cases on narrower grounds.

One example involved a Georgia statute prohibiting the publication of a rape victim's identity. In the case of a young woman who was raped and murdered, a court clerk allowed a television reporter to see an indictment that included the name of the victim—which was then broadcast. The victim's father sued the broadcaster for publication of private facts. When this case, *Cox Broadcasting v. Cohn* (1975), went to the Supreme Court, the broadcast company argued that the state statute barring its use of the victim's name violated the First Amendment. But the Court did not reach that question. It held that the broadcaster could not be penalized because it had obtained the name from public records, the document shown to the reporter by the court clerk. Justice Byron R. White wrote: "By placing the information in the official court records the State must be presumed to have concluded that the public interest was thereby being served." I find that assertion of Justice White's puzzling. Why would the action of a court clerk—very likely a mistake on his or her part—be taken as more indicative of Georgia's policy than the state statute finding that it was not in the public interest to publish the name of rape victims? To avoid a hard question, the Supreme Court seems to have engaged in judicial sleight-of-hand.

Cox Broadcasting v. Cohn was followed by other cases in which newspapers published matters that state statutes had required to be kept confidential: the name of a state judge whom a state commission considered investigating, the names of juvenile offenders, and again the name of a rape victim. In each case, the Supreme Court declined to adopt a general rule that such statutes violated the First Amendment; instead it found particular circumstances, every time, that freed the newspaper from the consequences of noncompliance. One's conclusion had to be that the Supreme Court was not greatly moved by the interests of privacy, even when those interests were embraced in state statutes.

Then, in 2001, the Supreme Court dealt with a federal law protecting the privacy of telephone and other conversations. The Omnibus Crime Control and Safe Streets Act of 1968 made it a crime to intercept such conversations or to disclose what was intercepted. The law also allowed civil damage suits for interceptions. In the case before the Court, *Bartnicki v. Vopper*, someone unknown taped a cell-phone call between two union officers in Pennsylvania during a strike. One said to the other: "If they're not gonna move for 3 percent, we're gonna have to go to their, their homes. . . . To blow off their front porches. . . . " The unknown intercepter sent the tape to a union opponent, who gave it to a radio station. The tape was played on the radio.

The union officers who were taped sued the radio station for damages. In the Supreme Court, the broadcaster argued that the law against disclosure of illegally taped conversations had to yield to the station's interest, protected by the First Amendment, in broadcasting the tape. A divided Supreme Court decided in favor of the broadcaster. Justice John Paul Stevens, in an opinion for a six-justice majority, gave short shrift to the privacy interests. But two of the six, justices Stephen Breyer and Sandra Day O'Connor, joined in a separate concurring opinion, written by Breyer, that gave much greater weight to the privacy claim.

Discussing the importance of privacy, Justice Breyer made a novel point. Giving people an assurance of privacy not only protects "the right to be let alone," he said, but encourages them to speak freely: It "helps to overcome our natural reluctance to discuss private matters when we fear that our private conversations may become public. And the statutory restrictions consequently encourage conversations that otherwise might not take place." In other words, there is a free-speech argument for protecting the privacy of conversations. Justice Breyer indicated that he and Justice O'Connor joined Justice Stevens here only because the intercepted call involved a matter of "unusual public concern, namely a threat of physical harm."

The Breyer opinion suggests that American law may yet put limits on the crushing of privacy in the name of freedom. We are in the age of exposure now: self-exposure on television, exposure of every kind of human fault or flaw by the press, tabloid and otherwise. We have come a long way from the modest indignity that provoked Brandeis's great defense of privacy, the use of pictures of his partner's wife without her consent. Not only the press but the law itself mercilessly exposes private lives. Kenneth Starr, the independent counsel who tried to drive President Bill Clinton from office, used his power to obtain Monica Lewinsky's letters and personal jottings from her personal computer—and included them in the report he sent to the House of Representatives. Despite Lewinsky's plea, he also included in the report computer messages Lewinsky had received from a woman friend telling about conflict with her husband. Starr issued a subpoena demanding that a Washington bookstore produce a record of all the books Lewinsky had bought there.

When Judge Charles Clark rejected William Sidis's privacy suit, he said he could imagine situations in which a "public character" like Sidis could succeed in getting damages for violation of his privacy: if "revelations" were so "intimate and unwarranted . . . as to outrage the community's notions of decency." Nowadays it is hard to imagine any revelation so intimate that it would offend the public's sense of decency.

The press is right that judges must not let their disapproval of rancid journalism lead them to censor anything that offends them. An English judge, Lord Chief Justice Woolf, got it right in 2002 when he set aside an injunction obtained by a football player to keep a tabloid newspaper from telling the story of his extramarital sexual relations with two women. Courts "should not act as censors or arbiters of taste," Lord Woolf said. "The fact that a more lurid approach will be adopted by the publication than the court would regard as acceptable is not relevant." Moreover, he said, a man who indulges in multiple affairs cannot complain if one of the women kisses and tells. Lord Woolf added: "The courts must not ignore the fact that if newspapers do not publish information which the public are interested in, there will be fewer newspapers published, which will not be in the public interest." British courts in the past had been all too ready to stop the press, so Lord Woolf's judgment marked a change—a step, one might say, toward the First Amendment's premise of an open society.

But it does not follow—not for me, at any rate—that an open society must allow the publication of private facts no matter how cruel or antisocial the publication would be. The reason was well expressed by Professor Thomas Nagel of New York University:

> The distinction between what an individual exposes to public view and what he conceals or exposes only to intimates is essential to permit creatures as complex as ourselves to interact without constant social breakdown. Each of our inner lives is such a jungle of thoughts, feelings, fantasies and impulses that civilization would be impossible if we expressed them all. . . . Just as social life would be impossible if we expressed all our lustful, aggressive, greedy, anxious or self-obsessed feelings in ordinary public encounters, so would inner life be impossible if we tried to become wholly persons whose thoughts, feelings and private behavior could be safely exposed to public view.

Secrecy is a red flag to journalists, rightly so. Governments use it to hide corruption and incompetence and to increase their unaccountable power. Their power has grown enormously. But a substantial part of it is the power to intrude in the lives of citizens by electronic and other means that were unimaginable to Brandeis when he predicted in his wiretapping dissent in 1928 that the state would find methods even more intrusive than wiretapping. When the press joins the government in intruding on privacy, it is not playing its essential role as a check on the power of the state.

When Czechoslovakia was under Communist control, the police secretly recorded the conversations of a leading dissident, Jan Prochazka, with another dissident friend. One day the state radio began broadcasting the tapes. The great Czech writer Milan Kundera said the tactic nearly succeeded in its purpose of denigrating Prochazka. People were shocked, Kundera said, because "in private a person says all sorts of things, uses coarse language, acts silly, tells dirty jokes . . . floats heretical ideas he'd never admit in public and so forth." But gradually people realized, Kundera wrote, "that the real scandal was not Prochazka's daring talk but the rape of his life; they realized, as if by electric shock, that private and public are two essentially different worlds and that respect for the difference is the indispensable condition, the sine qua non, for a man to live free. . . . "

In an interview in 1985, Kundera summed up his views on privacy:

We live in an age when private life is being destroyed. The police destroy it in Communist countries, journalists threaten it in democratic countries, and little by little the people themselves lose their taste for private life and their sense of it. Life when one can't hide from the eyes of others—that is hell. Those who have lived in totalitarian countries know it, but that system only brings out, like a magnifying glass, the tendencies of all modern society. . . . Without secrecy, nothing is possible—not love, not friendship.

The First Amendment's guarantees of freedom of speech and of the press are fundamentals of our freedom, but they are not the only essentials of a healthy society. If they succeed in totally overriding the interest of privacy, it would be a terrible victory.

6

A Press Privilege?

M arie Torre was a television columnist for the *New York Herald Tribune* in the 1950s. In 1957 she wrote a column about Judy Garland, the great stage and movie star, that made First Amendment history. Garland had signed a contract with the CBS television network to do a series of specials, but she was proving evasive about setting a date for the first program. The Torre column said a CBS executive, unnamed, had told Torre that something was bothering Garland—"I don't know, but I wouldn't be surprised if it's because she thinks she's terribly fat." Later biographies said Garland was in fact overweight at the time and was taking too many diet pills.

Judy Garland sued CBS for libel and breach of contract, seeking $1.4 million in damages. In pretrial proceedings, her lawyers demanded that Torre name the CBS executive who was the alleged source of the quotation. She refused to do so, saying that if she did, "nobody in the business will talk to me again." A federal judge held her in contempt and ordered her to serve ten days in prison. She appealed to the United States Court of Appeals for the Second Circuit.

Torre's lawyers argued that the First Amendment protected her against having to disclose her source—gave her a testimonial privilege, in the language of the law—because breaking her promise of confidentiality to the source would, as she said, curdle her relations with other potential sources. It was the first time that constitutional argument had ever been made: the beginning of what has become a familiar legal debate about the rights of journalists. The outcome in the Torre case was a preview of the ultimate fate of the claim that journalists have a constitutional privilege unavailable to others.

The opinion on appeal was written by a judge visiting from the Sixth Federal Circuit, Potter Stewart, who later became a Supreme Court justice. He said he accepted "the hypothesis that compulsory disclosure of a journalist's confidential sources of information may entail an abridgment of press freedom by imposing some limitation upon the availability of news." But freedom of the press is not an absolute, Judge Stewart wrote. It "must give way under the Constitution to a paramount public interest in the fair administration of justice." Quoting an opinion in another case, he went on: "'The right to sue and defend in the courts is the alternative of force. In an organized society it is the right conservative of all other rights, and lies at the foundation of orderly government.'" And in this case, he said, the testimony demanded was not of "doubtful relevance"; it "went to the heart of the plaintiff's claim."

In that first exploration of the problem, Judge Stewart fairly laid out what have become the debating points ever since. Crucially, he made clear that the journalist's interest is not the only one to be considered. The press does have a real interest: that of maintaining an ability to use sources who will not speak to a reporter unless promised confidentiality. But on the other side in this kind of civil case, there is the interest of the person whose good name has been sullied. Would we want to deprive someone whose reputation has been trashed by an anonymous source of any real chance of repairing that reputation in court? I would not.

Marie Torre asked the Supreme Court to hear the case, but it refused. She went to jail for ten days, still refusing to name her source. Then Judy Garland dropped the case. Why? Perhaps she had developed sympathy for Torre. Or perhaps she decided that the publicity over the litigation was making her look bad.

The Supreme Court took up the issue of reporter's privilege, as it had come to be called, in 1972. It agreed to review three cases in which reporters had been subpoenaed to appear or testify before grand juries in criminal proceedings, and had refused to do so. The decision took the name of the first case, *Branzburg v. Hayes*. Paul Branzburg, a reporter on the *Courier-Journal* of Louisville, Kentucky, had written an article describing young people synthesizing hashish. State authorities wanted to know their names.

By a vote of 5 to 4, the Supreme Court rejected the reporters' claims. Justice Byron R. White wrote the opinion of the Court, beginning with a flat statement of the result. "The issue in these cases," he said, "is whether requiring newsmen to appear and testify before state or federal grand juries abridges the freedom of speech and press guaranteed by the First Amendment. We hold that it does not."

Justice White made what seemed a reluctant concession, expressed in a double negative, to the press argument. He did not suggest, he said, "that news gathering does not qualify for First Amendment protection; without some protection for seeking out the news, freedom of the press could be eviscerated." But he went on to point out that while the First Amendment protected the press from prior restraints and subsequent penalties for what it published, the press was also traditionally barred from many sources of news. "Despite the fact that news gathering may be hampered," he wrote, "the press is regularly excluded from grand jury proceedings, our own conferences, the meetings of other official bodies gathered in executive session. . . . " The obligation to testify is critical to the functioning of our criminal justice system, he said, and exceptions to that duty are frowned upon. He added a historical note: that Chief Justice John Marshall, in 1807, "opined that in historical circumstances a subpoena could be issued to the President of the United States." (The *Branzburg* case was decided on June 29, 1972—twelve days after the break-in at the Watergate that led eventually to a subpoena for President Nixon's tapes and then his resignation from office.)

Practical reasons against granting a constitutional privilege to the press were also advanced by Justice White. One was the difficulty of defining who counts as "the press" and thus would qualify for the privilege. The traditional idea, Justice White said, is that "liberty of the press is the right of the lonely pamphleteer . . . just as much as of the large metropolitan publisher." How would courts define those who were entitled to the privilege? (This concern has become far more compelling since then, with the rise of the Internet and millions of bloggers who circulate what they may regard as news.) Justice White went on to make a related point:

> The informative function asserted by representatives of the organized press in the present cases is also performed by lecturers, political pollsters, novelists, academic researchers, and dramatists. Almost any author may quite accurately assert that he is contributing to the flow of information to the public, that he relies on confidential sources of information, and that these sources will be silenced if he is forced to make disclosures before a grand jury.

Again, the concern expressed by Justice White has been borne out. In a postlude to the Pentagon Papers case the Nixon administration subpoenaed an assistant professor of government at Harvard, Samuel Popkin, to appear before a grand jury and identify sources for a scholarly paper he had written on Vietnam. He refused—and went to jail for a week. The president of Harvard, Derek Bok, then appeared as his lawyer and embarrassed the government into ending the grand jury term and thus freeing Popkin.

There was a skeptical tone at places in Justice White's *Branzburg* opinion. The press "is far from helpless to protect itself from harassment or substantial harm," he said; it "has at its disposal powerful mechanisms of communication." But the opinion ended with what may have been meant as a reassuring note, expressed in another double negative: "News gathering is not without its First Amendment protections," Justice White said, "and grand jury investigations if instituted or conducted other than in good faith, would pose wholly different issues for resolution under the First Amendment."

In the *Branzburg* case the press did not seek an absolute privilege for journalists: one that would protect them from having to testify before grand juries in all circumstances. A brief filed by the *New York Times* explained that a subpoena should not be enforced against a journalist unless: (1) the government showed there was probable cause to believe the journalist had information relevant to a specific probable crime; (2) the government showed that it could not obtain the information from other sources; and (3) the government showed "a compelling and overriding interest in the information."

Three justices, dissenting, would have given journalists a qualified privilege against having to testify by imposing those three requirements on governments. The opinion was by Justice Stewart, who denounced what he called the majority's "crabbed view of the First Amendment," which he said "reflects a disturbing insensitivity to the critical role of an independent press in our society." As a Sixth Circuit judge, Stewart had required Marie Torre to identify the unnamed CBS source of the defamatory comment on Judy Garland; to some, that may have seemed inconsistent with his dissenting opinion in *Branzburg*. Justice Stewart merely noted the *Garland* case in a footnote, quoting the statement in his *Garland* opinion that the demand for the source's name "went to the heart of the plaintiff's claim." Perhaps he meant that, if something like the qualified privilege test were applied in a civil case, Judy Garland had met the test because she could not get the critical information from anyone other than Marie Torre. The fourth dissenter, Justice William O. Douglas, would have given journalists an absolute First Amendment privilege against having to testify before a grand jury unless they were themselves involved in a crime. Justice Douglas denounced the *Times* for taking what he called "the amazing position that First Amendment rights are to be balanced against other needs or conveniences of government." The Framers of the First Amendment cast it "in absolute terms," he said, not "the timid, watered-down, emasculated versions of the First Amendment which both the Government and The New York Times advance."

The *Branzburg* decision was the Supreme Court's first judgment on the press privilege claim, and the last for decades. As of 2007, the Court has not agreed to hear another case raising the issue. And so, one would think, the question was settled. Wrong. Far from it, in fact. Over the decades, journalists in a variety of situations declined to disclose their confidential sources—and continued to claim that the First Amendment gave them that privilege. Sometimes lower courts agreed with them, sometimes not. It was an extraordinary legal pattern. A Supreme Court decision that was evidently meant to be the last word on a problem was being widely ignored or explained away.

Why? One reason was that one of the five justices in the *Branzburg* majority, Lewis F. Powell Jr., wrote a brief opinion of his own. He joined the opinion of the Court by Justice

White and rejected the journalists' claims in the three cases before the Court. But Justice Powell said journalists could still challenge orders to testify in other cases: "if a newsman believes that the grand jury investigation is not being conducted in good faith," for example, or if the information sought from him bears "only a remote and tenuous relationship to the subject of the investigation." That sounded a good deal like the qualified privilege that Justice Stewart proposed in dissent. And Justice Powell said judges should balance freedom of the press and the need for testimony in criminal matters "on a case-by-case basis."

Many lower courts, state and federal, read Powell's concurring opinion as effectively modifying Justice White's flat rejection of the journalists' privilege claim. In civil cases especially, judges accepted his invitation to weigh the interests of press confidentiality and the need for the information case by case.

There was another reason for the peculiar status of the *Branzburg* decision. The press simply did not accept it. Editors and publishers, and their lawyers, spoke of "the First Amendment privilege" against compelled disclosure of sources as if that privilege existed. In 1981, for example, a *Washington Post* story that won the Pulitzer Prize—a story about an eight-year-old heroin addict in the Washington, D.C., slums—turned out to have been fabricated. When the hoax was discovered, an editorial in the *Post* warned against using the episode "to discredit the various First Amendment protections that were activated . . . when the conflict sharpened between the paper and the authorities on the question of identification of sources." Translated, that remarkable statement meant that the Washington police and other authorities looking into the supposed crime of hooking an eight-year-old on heroin were prevented by the First Amendment from pressing the reporter for the real names of the characters in her story. It is hard to believe that any court, even one using the balancing test, would go that far.

But the press's privilege claims were not usually as absurd as the one made about the fraudulent *Washington Post* story. Some of the most important work journalists do can only be accomplished by relying on confidential sources. That was dramatically so, for example, when the *New York Times* in 2005 reported that President George W. Bush had ordered the National Security Agency to tap international telephone calls without obtaining the warrants required by law. It was a vitally important story, bringing to light—and to a degree of accountability—a lawless executive activity. And of course the facts could only have come from confidential sources inside the government. The response of the government was a threat to subpoena the reporters who wrote the story and demand the names of the sources: that is, to focus on the leak instead of the flagrant violation of law in the program that the story exposed.

The last half of the twentieth century and the first years of the twenty-first saw a vast growth of executive power in the United States, very often exercised in secret, without scrutiny by Congress. President Bush claimed the unilateral power not only to eavesdrop on American citizens but to imprison them forever without trial on suspicion of being "enemy combatants." The press, with all its defects, is often the only defense against the abuse of power. Watergate was a signal example—

and that exposure of the Nixon administration's abuses depended famously on unnamed sources.

If a journalist promises to keep a source's name confidential, he or she absolutely has to keep that promise. That is an ethical demand, and one of common sense: As Marie Torre understood, who will talk to you in the future if you break a promise? Disclosing a name that you undertook to keep secret can also have legal consequences. When a Republican operative told reporters for Minnesota newspapers that the Democratic candidate for lieutenant governor had a criminal record, the newspapers published the story and—despite a promise to keep his name secret—disclosed the source. The source sued for violation of the promise. The newspapers argued that it would violate the First Amendment to make them pay damages, but the Supreme Court rejected that argument in a 1991 decision.

The clash between journalists' need to keep their promises of confidentiality and court orders to name their sources occasionally produces a dramatic denouement: a writer going to prison for contempt of court. An extreme example was the case of Vanessa Leggett, a Texas woman who had never published anything but set out to write a book about a notorious murder. After she had conducted many interviews, a federal grand jury subpoenaed her and demanded her notes and the names of her sources. She said no—and spent 168 days in jail for contempt.

Vanessa Leggett was not a journalist. That is an embarrassing fact for the editors and press lawyers who say the First Amendment should be read to provide a testimonial privilege for journalists. They feel uncomfortable about excluding

Leggett from their legal theory, as well they should. But including such writers would bring them back to the problem Justice White foresaw in his *Branzburg* opinion: the difficulty of defining who is to qualify for a journalists' privilege. White said freedom was as much for "the lonely pamphleteer" as for the *New York Times* reporter. Bloggers, in all their millions, are the modern version of lonely pamphleteers. Vanessa Leggett surely qualified as the purveyor of information to the public. But if the courts are to define, case by case, who qualifies for a testimonial privilege and who does not, then judges will be issuing something like journalists' licenses—which are required in some countries but are utter anathema to the American press, which rightly regards press licensing as a form of official control.

The press, unable to get assured protection from subpoenas through its First Amendment argument in the courts, has pushed for statutes giving journalists a testimonial privilege. Almost all states have adopted such shield laws, as they are called. (The state laws do not apply in federal courts, where some of the most controversial privilege cases have arisen.)

Shield laws do not dispose of all the doubts about exempting journalists from the universal citizens' duty to testify in court when called. Those doubts are illustrated by the case of Wen Ho Lee, a scientist at the Los Alamos National Laboratory who was described in various press stories in the late 1990s as an atomic spy. The stories, evidently the result of leaks from government sources, said Lee was suspected of giving secrets to China. He was arrested, charged with fifty-nine felony counts, and held for nine months in solitary confinement.

Then the government dropped all but one of the counts, a charge that he mishandled information that had been retroactively classified as "secret." The judge handling the case apologized to Lee and said officials had "embarrassed our entire nation and each of us who is a citizen of it." A *Boston Globe* editorial said the suspicions about Lee came from an intelligence official "with a reputation for right-wing zealotry and racist behavior."

Lee sued the government for violation of his privacy in the leaks to the press. His lawyers subpoenaed five reporters and asked about the sources of their stories. They refused to answer, and they were held in contempt and ordered to pay fines of $500 a day until they agreed to respond. Then five news organizations—ABC News, the *Los Angeles Times*, the *New York Times*, the *Washington Post*, and the Associated Press—settled the case and ended the contempt sanctions by agreeing to pay Lee $750,000. The government also contributed $895,000 toward his lawyers' fees and taxes.

In settling the case, the news organizations made no apology for their contemptible treatment of Wen Ho Lee. They said they agreed to settle "to protect our journalists from further sanctions" and to protect their ability to obtain information that can come "only from confidential sources." In other words: We don't care what we did to Wen Ho Lee; we care only about our needs. The *Boston Globe*, which had not been part of the attack on Lee, saw the real situation in an editorial on the settlement. It said: "It is important to remember what was done to Lee because powerful institutions rarely admit abuse of their powers, and because the rule of law is imperiled when the government and a compliant or gullible press tramples on the rights of a single private citizen."

Suppose that a federal shield law had existed when Wen Ho Lee sued to seek some compensation for his nightmare ordeal. The journalists who wrote the damaging stories would have had their subpoenas dismissed, and without the names of the leakers Lee would probably have had to give up his lawsuit. Is that what a decent society should want? Would that have really benefited the press? Or would it have added to the evident public feeling that the press is arrogant, demanding special treatment?

The press, as James Madison told us long ago, can be a crucial force in countering abuse of official power. But it is not always the good guy. It can be a compliant or gullible handmaiden of government abuse. Or it can be something even worse, as a South African case shows.

During the time of racial oppression in South Africa, a news magazine called *To the Point* published an article about a black minister, the Reverend Dr. Manas Buthelezi. It said that while he spoke publicly of the need for peaceful change, according to "reliable sources" he privately advocated "violence." That was an extremely damaging charge in apartheid South Africa, one that could have brought Dr. Buthelezi's imprisonment or even execution. He sued *To the Point* for libel—and demanded to know the names of the "reliable sources." The editor claimed a privilege to keep them secret. The court rejected the claim and decided the case in favor of Dr. Buthelezi, awarding him damages. Some time later, in what South Africans called the "Information Scandal," disclosures from the Ministry of Information showed that the article in *To the Point* had actually been written by the secret police.

When an American public figure sues for libel after a devastating attack, the Supreme Court's libel rule requires him or her to prove that the author of the charge made it knowing that it was false or in reckless disregard of its truth or falsity. That gives great protection to the press. It really means that the victim must find out what the author knew before publishing. If journalists were immunized from having to respond to questions, the injured person would essentially be stymied. Someone whose life was ruined by a false report could not sue successfully to repair his or her reputation. That should not be an acceptable result in a civilized society. The press, having won great protection in libel cases, cannot expect to have a testimonial privilege in those cases as well.

The solution in libel suits is not to put a journalist in jail if he or she refuses to name the confidential source who made a charge against the plaintiff. It is for the judge to tell the jury that it can assume there was no such source. That formula would effectively force the press to have at least one named source for any pejorative story, or be prepared to pay libel damages if sued. Such an approach has been used in a number of states.

When a journalist's testimony becomes an issue in criminal prosecutions, it is usually the prosecutor who wants the testimony. But it can be the defendant, and then our sense of what justice requires may be different. If a reporter has confidential information that could help a defendant charged with murder, can he or she properly withhold it?

Something like that scenario played out in the case of Myron Farber, a *New York Times* reporter. In 1975 Farber wrote a series of articles about deaths in a Hackensack, New Jersey, hospital—deaths that were unexplained. The articles said that a doctor in the hospital—Farber called him Doctor X, withholding the name—had murdered five patients with the poison curare. New Jersey authorities reopened their investigation of the deaths and indicted a surgeon, Dr. Mario Jascalevich. Jascalevich's lawyer subpoenaed Farber's notes, arguing that they could show inconsistencies between what his sources had said to him and what they might say on the stand. The judge ordered Farber to provide the notes—and, when he refused to, sentenced him to six months in jail for contempt. The *Times* had to pay a fine of $100,000 plus $5,000 a day while the subpoena was defied. New Jersey had a journalists' shield law, and Farber relied on it. But the state supreme court held that it had to yield to the defendant's constitutional right to evidence.

After Farber spent forty days in prison, he was pardoned by the governor of New Jersey, Brendan Byrne, who also returned $286,000 that the *Times* had paid in fines. There was no doubt that Myron Farber had taken his stand on principle, and the chance of the defendant's lawyer actually finding something useful in his notes seemed rather remote. But it is easy to see that in an appropriate case it would be morally testing for a journalist to withhold information from a criminal defendant.

The truth is that there are ethical and other compelling interests on both sides of the privilege issue. The press does need to use confidential informants; sometimes parties seeking

to clear their names—a Wen Ho Lee, a Manas Buthelezi—
have an indisputable reason. The fact that there are interests
on both sides should make journalists be cautious in relying on
unnamed sources in what they write. For one thing, it is
plainly wrong to quote anonymous sources in pejorative comments on individuals. ("The mayor has taken bribes in his office," an informed source told the *Daily Bugle*.) That is not just
unfair to the mayor; it is asking for a confrontation over a demand for the name of the "informed source" if the mayor sues.
The press has come to understand the possibility of abuse in
using unnamed sources. The *New York Times*, for example, has
internal rules requiring that an editor be told the reason for
the confidentiality, and specifically barring the use of anonymous pejorative comments.

Thirty-five years after the *Branzburg* decision it is clear
that the First Amendment is not going to provide a solution
to the conflict between the press's need for confidential
sources and the occasional need of the legal process for journalists' evidence. In a number of high-profile cases lower
courts have rejected the press's constitutional arguments. The
Supreme Court has shown no interest in reexamining the
issue; the chance that it will read the First Amendment to give
journalists a testimonial privilege is zero.

The trouble with the constitutional claim is that it fits awk-
wardly with the general course of First Amendment decisions
on the freedom of the press. Starting in 1931, the Supreme
Court largely immunized the press from prior restraints (in
Near v. Minnesota) and subsequent penalties for what it published (in *New York Times v. Sullivan*). It hardly ever read the

First Amendment as assuring the acquisition of information, and then only when the complaint was against closed courtrooms. And in those courtroom cases the Supreme Court gave no special access to the press, deciding rather that courtrooms must be open to the public at large. To prevail with its constitutional argument on the privilege issue, the press would have to persuade the Supreme Court to take two new steps: First, it would have to decide that the First Amendment gives the press (however defined) access to information not given to the public, and then it would have to decide that keeping sources secret is crucial to that access.

Journalists and their lawyers often speak as if the First Amendment, in guaranteeing the freedom of "the press," protected an institution—the organized press. Indeed, Justice Stewart made that assumption in a lecture. But in the eighteenth century there was nothing like the organized press institutions that developed later. In promising "the freedom of speech, or of the press," the amendment surely meant merely to cover both oral and written expression: pamphlets and books just as much as newspapers. Once the premise of a specially protected institution is put aside, the constitutional claim for special treatment of journalists in the courts becomes more difficult to sustain.

All this suggests that the question of a testimonial privilege for journalists is really one of public policy rather than of constitutional law. The Constitution did not create the privileges familiar in Anglo-American law: the assurances that a lawyer need not testify against a client, a doctor against a patient, one spouse against another. They were adopted by courts and legislatures in response to felt needs. In 1975 Congress formalized the process for federal courts by explicitly authorizing them to develop privileges in keeping with "the principles of the common law as they may be interpreted . . . in the light of reason and experience." Under that authority, the Supreme Court recognized privileges for communications between lawyers and clients, wives and husbands, psychotherapists and patients.

In 2005 a judge of the United States Court of Appeals for the District of Columbia Circuit, David Tatel, proposed that the federal courts use the authority of the 1975 statute to adopt a qualified privilege for journalists. He said "reason and experience" called for that step because the press had such an important role in exposing official abuse of power and because forty-nine states (all but Wyoming) had adopted some form of press privilege by statute or judicial decision.

Judge Tatel spoke of the "clash between two truth-seeking institutions: the grand jury and the press." He suggested a qualified privilege that would balance interests, but one different from the three-part test advocated by Justice Stewart in dissent in the *Branzburg* case. The latter would not work when the government was seeking the source of a leak, he pointed out; the only people who would know would be the leaker and the journalist, so the government could always show that it had no alternative witnesses. Instead, Judge Tatel said, courts should balance the interest in compelling disclosure, measured by the harm the leak caused, against the public interest in newsgathering, measured by the leaked information's value. Thus, for example, if the government wanted to learn who leaked the

story of President Bush's order for wiretapping without required warrants, a court would weigh the harm caused by that
leak against the importance of the information to the public. In
my view the latter would plainly prevail, and the reporters
would have a privilege not to disclose their source.

Judge Tatel's qualified privilege would not assure a victory
for the press every time, not at all. That was clear from the
very case in which he put forward his idea: the contempt proceedings against Judith Miller of the *New York Times* and Matt
Cooper of *Time* magazine. The underlying issue there was a
leak about Iraq's supposed weapons of mass destruction. In a
speech in 2003, President Bush said Saddam Hussein's deter-
mination to have those weapons was shown by an intelligence
report saying that Iraq was trying to buy uranium ore in Niger,
in Africa. On July 6, 2003, the *Times* published an op-ed piece
by Joseph Wilson, a former ambassador, saying that he had
been sent to Niger to investigate that report and found it false.
His article infuriated the Bush administration. Soon Robert
Novak, a conservative columnist, wrote that high sources had
told him that Wilson's wife, Valerie Plame Wilson, was a secret agent at the CIA and had suggested he be sent on that
mission. It can be a crime to disclose the name of a secret intelligence agent. A special prosecutor was appointed to investigate. He called Miller and Cooper before a grand jury to
testify on who had told them about Wilson and Plame; they
refused to answer. Cooper eventually did reply, but Miller
spent eighty-five days in jail before she said she had permission
from her source to give his name—Lewis Libby, chief of staff
to Vice President Dick Cheney. She was then released.

When the contempt orders were before the Court of Appeals, on appeal by Miller and Cooper, Judge Tatel proposed his idea of the court adopting a qualified privilege. His colleagues did not agree with him, but he wrote an opinion applying his proposal to the facts of this case—and concluded that there should be no testimonial privilege for the two journalists. On the one hand, he said, what was leaked—the name of an intelligence agent—was a serious matter, possibly even criminal. On the other, the news value of Valerie Plame's name and employment was "marginal."

David Tatel had a high reputation as a judge, including a particular sensitivity to First Amendment interests. The press and its lawyers could not persuasively dismiss his opinion as the product of bias or unfairness. The press might better have taken the case as a warning against pressing its claims too far and separating itself from the mainstream of the law and public opinion.

A warning against doing that had come, years before, from one of the press's greatest friends, Justice William J. Brennan Jr. of the Supreme Court. In 1979, when press organizations had lost a case in the Supreme Court and cried out that the Constitution was unraveling, he urged them to be more careful and more understanding in their claims. He added: "This may involve a certain loss of innocence, a certain recognition that the press, like other institutions, must accommodate a variety of important social interests."

7

Fear Itself

Early in 1918, the year after the United States entered World War I, Montana adopted a state sedition law. The act made it a crime, punishable by a fine of up to $20,000 and a prison term of up to twenty years, to "utter, print, write, or publish any disloyal, profane, violent, scurrilous, contemptuous, slurring, or abusive language" in wartime about the government, the Constitution, the flag, or the military uniforms of the United States, or to say anything calculated to bring them "into contempt, scorn, contumely, or disrepute."

In the next year, seventy-nine Montanans were convicted of violating that vague language. A real estate man was convicted for having said, "Because I don't buy Liberty Bonds and don't carry the goddamn flag they call me pro-German." A sheep rancher was convicted after being accused by tenants he had been trying to evict. A traveling salesman for a wine company was found guilty for having called wartime food regulations "a big joke." He was sentenced to from seven and one-half to twenty years at hard labor. Many of the convictions were for comments made in saloons.

State and local committees enforced their ideas of patriotism. The Montana Council of Defense issued an order forbidding the use of the German language in schools and churches. (Montana had some communities of German origin.) In Lewistown a mob went into the high school, took all the German textbooks, and burned them in the street. Newspapers worked up fear of German plots. The editor of the *Helena Independent*, Will Campbell, warned against poisonous beans being sneaked into the country; after hearing about tales of mysterious airplane sightings, he wrote, "Are the Germans about to bomb the capital of Montana?"

Montana, so far from the war in Europe, might have been thought the last place to be gripped by fear of The Enemy. Its unlikely record was forgotten until it was unearthed in a book published in 2005: *Darkest Before Dawn: Sedition and Free Speech in the American West*, by Clemens P. Work of the School of Journalism at the University of Montana in Missoula. I have taken my examples from him. The book had an extraordinary consequence. Law students in a class at the university looked into the sedition cases, got in touch with family members of those who were convicted, and helped draft a pardon petition. In May 2006 Governor Brian Schweitzer posthumously pardoned seventy-eight Montanans convicted of sedition under the 1918 law. (One had been pardoned earlier.) Schweitzer made a statement that he said should have been made by the governor who proposed the law, Sam Stewart: "I'm sorry, forgive me and God bless America, because we can criticize our government."

The patriotic hysteria in Montana during World War I was a sample of a national phenomenon. In fact, the Montana sedition law was used as the model for a federal Sedition Act—the first since 1798—passed by Congress at the urging of President Wilson. The federal law differed from Montana's in only three insignificant words. It was the statute used against the radicals who threw pamphlets from a rooftop in New York City in *Abrams v. United States*, in which Justice Holmes wrote his first, memorable free-speech dissent. ("It is an experiment, as all life is an experiment.")

The federal Sedition Act and the wartime statute it amended, the Espionage Act of 1917, swept up all kinds of obscure victims apart from those known to us because the Supreme Court considered their cases. Clemens Work's book cites the case of Clarence Waldron, a Pentecostal minister in Windsor, Vermont, who was prosecuted for telling his Bible class that "a Christian can take no part in the war" and "Don't shed your precious blood for your country." The jury found that his words showed an intent to "cause insubordination, disloyalty, or refusal of duty." He was convicted and sentenced to fifteen years in prison. More than 2,000 Americans, most of them no more dangerous than Clarence Waldron, were prosecuted under the Espionage and Sedition Acts.

It is a seeming characteristic of American society that it is periodically gripped by fear—fear manipulated by politicians. In 1798 it was French Jacobin terrorists who were supposedly going to infiltrate; even someone as sensible as Abigail Adams was touched by that fear. In the middle of the nineteenth century the Know-Nothing Party warned against the dire influence of immigrant Roman Catholics. After World War I demagogues persuaded many Americans that they were in mortal danger from political radicals.

Of course no society is immune from the poison of fear. Germany was a country of high culture, and Jews had an important place in it, before it was taken over by an anti-Semitic mass murderer. But America, though it has faced economic troubles more than once, has never experienced anything like the distress of Weimar Germany. With its continental reach and vast resources, it might have been expected to be less susceptible to panic. That proved untrue time and again. Even in a time of strong economic growth, the years after World War II, another Red Scare developed. Congressional committees hunted Communists with considerable public support: a phenomenon that reached its peak in the 1950s in the maestro of fear and hate, Senator Joe McCarthy.

The excesses of patriotic fervor during America's participation in World War I were succeeded, after the war, by the outrages of the first American Red Scare. The Bolshevik Revolution in Russia aroused fear of all kinds of radicalism—fear of socialists, communists, anarchists. Industrialists saw the hand of revolutionaries in strikes, particularly in the activities of the feared radical union, the Industrial Workers of the World (IWW). Politicians played on the fear. Twenty states adopted legislation banning "criminal syndicalism." These laws made it a crime to join an organization with the doctrine of advocating violence for political ends—whether or not a defendant personally held those views or had acted on them. (California's Criminal Syndicalism Act was the one used against Anita Whitney in *Whitney v. California*, the case that evoked Brandeis's classic argument for freedom of speech.)

In 1919 the United States House of Representatives refused to seat Victor Berger, who had been elected in Wisconsin as a member of the Socialist Party. In 1920 the New York State Assembly unseated five elected Socialists. That action brought a powerful response from Charles Evans Hughes, former governor of New York and former Supreme Court justice who narrowly lost to Woodrow Wilson as the Republican candidate for president in 1916. (He was appointed chief justice in 1930.) Hughes said it was "a most serious mistake to proceed against masses of our citizens . . . by denying them the only resource of peaceful government; that is, action by the ballot box. . . . "

Woodrow Wilson, who ran as a progressive Democrat and introduced important economic reform measures as president, left an abysmal record on civil liberties—including freedom of speech and of the press. He proposed the repressive Espionage Act of 1917 and Sedition Act of 1918. He urged Congress to make it a crime to publish anything that might be useful to the enemy in wartime. (Congress rejected that proposal after a barrage of critical newspaper editorials.) His postmaster general, Albert Burleson, barred from the mails any publication that he deemed critical of the war effort. For example, he explained, "papers may not say that the Government is controlled by Wall Street or munitions manufacturers, or any other special interests."

But it was Wilson's attorney general, A. Mitchell Palmer, who put his mark on the era most dramatically. At his direction, Department of Justice agents conducted raids in November 1919 and again the following January, arresting more than 4,000 supposed radicals. The Palmer Raids, as they were called, targeted aliens, about 800 of whom were deported. The most famous may have been Emma Goldman, who sounded a bit like Charles Evans Hughes when she said at her deportation hearing: "The free expression of the hopes and aspirations of a people is the greatest and only safety in a sane society."

The First Amendment is meant to assure Americans that they can believe what they will and say what they believe. But repeatedly, in times of fear and stress, men and women have been hunted, humiliated, punished for their words and beliefs. We look to the courts to maintain our faithfulness to freedom. This book, like others, tends to chart the state of American liberty in judicial decisions. But courts have hardly been consistent guarantors of free speech.

Courts did nothing to restrain the harsh consequences of the Sedition Act of 1798. The law's constitutionality was never definitively resolved before it expired, but justices of the Supreme Court acting as trial judges enforced it with no sign of reluctance. It was Madison, Jefferson, and their supporters who made the libertarian case against the Sedition Act. They—politicians, not judges—persuaded the contemporary public, and history, that it violated our commitment to freedom. The courts did nothing to stop the Palmer Raids and other government repressions during and after

World War I. Policies gradually changed then because of the force of criticism by Charles Evans Hughes, Professor Zechariah Chafee, and other liberal-minded men and women. The established press, it should be noted, was not in the vanguard in the defense of freedom; it tended to echo the government. More leadership came from private organizations such as the American Civil Liberties Union, founded in 1920.

Judge Learned Hand spoke at a wartime rally for freedom in Central Park, New York, in 1944. His speech, entitled "The Spirit of Liberty," included this often-quoted passage: "I often wonder whether we do not rest our hopes too much upon constitutions, upon laws and upon courts. These are false hopes, believe me, these are false hopes. Liberty lies in the hearts of men and women; when it dies there, no constitution, no law, no court can save it; no constitution, no law, no court can even do much to help it. While it lies there it needs no constitution, no law, no court to save it."

Judge Hand's rhetoric was memorable, and there was a kernel of truth in what he said. A society that does not value freedom cannot be kept free by a court. But his words were a misleading overstatement. Modern history shows that courts can do much to help, by inspiring devotion to freedom. Holmes and Brandeis had neither sword nor purse, as Alexander Hamilton said of courts. But they had words, and their words played a significant part in American society's growing attachment to freedom of speech later in the twentieth century—in the fitful realization of the promise of the First Amendment.

Consider cases decided by the Supreme Court a dozen years apart, in 1925 and 1937. In 1925, the Court upheld the conviction of a radical in the case of *Gitlow v. New York*. Benjamin Gitlow was prosecuted for publishing the manifesto of a small left-wing group that called for mass action to bring about a "revolutionary dictatorship of the proletariat." There was no charge that he sought immediate revolution or violence. Justice Holmes, dissenting with Justice Brandeis, rested on his clear and present danger test. He said there was "no present danger of an attempt to overthrow the government by force on the part of the admittedly small minority who shared the defendant's views." Holmes continued:

> It is said that this manifesto was more than a theory, that it was an incitement. Every idea is an incitement. It offers itself for belief and if believed it is acted on unless some other belief outweighs it or some failure of energy stifles the movement at its birth. The only difference between the expression of an opinion and an incitement in the narrower sense is the speaker's enthusiasm for the result. Eloquence may set fire to reason. But whatever may be thought of the redundant discourse before us, it had no chance of starting a present conflagration. If in the long run the beliefs expressed in proletarian dictatorship are destined to be accepted by the dominant forces of the community, the only meaning of free speech is that they should be given their chance and have their way.

Holmes's astringent characterization of Gitlow's manifesto as a "redundant discourse" put this case—and others like it—

in realistic perspective. Benjamin Gitlow was not a threat to American society. Decades later, one can only wonder why the authorities bothered with him. The same was true of hundreds of prosecutions brought under state statutes like the Montana sedition law and the federal Espionage and Sedition Acts. But the majority of the Supreme Court was still fixed on upholding the convictions of radicals whose words might have a "tendency" of which they disapproved. (The *Gitlow* decision was in fact important for another reason. The majority opinion, by Justice Edward T. Sanford, for the first time accepted the argument that the First Amendment's protections of speech and press from federal repression were applied to the states by the Fourteenth Amendment. From then on, most of the development of First Amendment freedoms came in state cases.)

In 1937 the Supreme Court made two decisions that turned away from fear of radicalism. In *De Jonge v. Oregon*, Dirk De Jonge had been convicted of violating Oregon's criminal syndicalism law when he helped to conduct a meeting held under the auspices of the Communist Party. There was no charge that "criminal syndicalism" or violence was advocated at the meeting. The sole basis of the conviction was the fact that the Communist Party had called the meeting.

The Supreme Court unanimously reversed De Jonge's conviction. The opinion, by Chief Justice Hughes, did not take up the debate about whether there was a clear and present danger of some substantive evil. Instead, the chief justice focused on the general importance of freedom of speech and freedom of assembly, which is also protected by the First

Amendment. ("Congress shall make no law . . . abridging the freedom of speech, or of the press; or the right of the people peaceably to assemble, and to petition the Government for a redress of grievances.") Hughes wrote: "The right of peaceable assembly is a right cognate to those of free speech and free press and is equally fundamental. . . . Peaceable assembly for lawful discussions cannot be made a crime. The holding of meetings for peaceable political action cannot be proscribed. Those who assist in the conduct of such meetings cannot be branded as criminals on that score."

Dirk De Jonge was in a different legal situation from that of Benjamin Gitlow and the others who had lost all the early cases. But underneath those differences one can sense a change in judicial attitude, a much greater sensitivity to the demands of free expression. De Jonge would not have prevailed in 1919, when the *Abrams* case was decided over Holmes's dissent, or in 1927, when Anita Whitney's was.

The 1937 Court had greater difficulty in the case of *Herndon v. Lowry*, decided in favor of a free-speech claim by a vote of 5 to 4. Angelo Herndon was a black man who acted as an organizer for the Communist Party in Georgia: a role that must have required extraordinary courage. He was convicted of "attempt to incite insurrection" in violation of a Georgia law because of his place in the Communist Party. The party advocated "self-determination" for predominantly black areas of the South, but there was no evidence that Herndon had personally advocated this program or urged it on those he tried to enlist in the party.

Justice Owen J. Roberts, in the opinion of the Court, focused on the character of what Herndon had been shown to have said, or not shown. His "membership in the Communist Party and his solicitation of a few members," Roberts wrote, "wholly fail to establish an attempt to incite others to insurrection. In these circumstances, to make membership in the party and solicitation of members for that party a criminal offense, punishable by death, in the discretion of a jury, is an unwarranted invasion of the right of freedom of speech." The dissenting opinion, by Justice Willis Van Devanter, spoke of the vulnerability of Herndon's target audience: southern blacks. The literature he carried, Van Devanter wrote, was "largely directed to a people whose past and present circumstances would lead them to give unusual credence to its inflaming and inciting features."

The two 1937 cases, *De Jonge* and *Herndon*, show how the fear of radical ideology that dominated the earlier decisions had ebbed as an influence in the Court—and freedom of speech had been given pride of place. One other case should be mentioned as an indication of how far the ideal of free speech had gone: *Cantwell v. Connecticut*, decided in 1940. An itinerant Jehovah's Witness preacher was convicted of breach of the peace when he denounced the Roman Catholic Church in a largely Catholic neighborhood. The case did not involve fear of radical doctrine; the legal issue was different. But Justice Roberts, in the opinion reversing the conviction, made plain where free speech now stood in the Court's hierarchy of interests:

In the realm of religious faith, and in that of political belief, sharp differences arise. In both fields the tenets of one man may seem the rankest error to his neighbor. To persuade others to his own point of view, the pleader, as we know, at times resorts to exaggeration, to vilification of men who have been, or are, prominent in church or state, and even to false statement. But the people of this nation have ordained in the light of history that, in spite of the probability of excesses and abuses, these liberties are, in the long view, essential to enlightened opinion and right conduct on the part of the citizens of a democracy.

World War II was a far more menacing conflict for the United States than World War I had been. A significant part of the American fleet was destroyed at the outset in the surprise Japanese attack on Pearl Harbor on December 7, 1941. Soon after that, President Franklin D. Roosevelt set in motion what was very likely the greatest blow to constitutional rights in all the wars and times of stress in American history. He authorized military commanders to exclude from the West Coast all persons of Japanese ancestry. About 120,000 people were removed from their homes on the coast, more than 80,000 of them American citizens, and confined behind barbed wire in desert "relocation camps." Why? Again, fear was the dominant reason—fear, spread by politicians, that Japan was about to invade the United States. Someone as profoundly humane as Earl Warren—then attorney general of California, later governor, and then chief justice of the United States—pressed for the removal because, he said, it was impossible to tell the difference between a loyal Japanese American and a disloyal one. In fact, not one was charged during the war with any form of disloyalty.

The Supreme Court made this civil-liberties disaster worse by refusing to pronounce it unlawful. In 1944, in *Korematsu v. United States*, the Court upheld the conviction of Fred Korematsu for being in California in violation of the military order. Justices Frank Murphy, Owen J. Roberts, and Robert H. Jackson dissented. Justice Jackson wrote:

> A military order, however unconstitutional, is not apt to last longer than the military emergency. [But] once a judicial opinion rationalizes such an order to show that it conforms to the Constitution, or rather rationalizes the Constitution to show that the Constitution sanctions such an order, the Court for all time has validated the principle of racial discrimination in criminal procedure and of transplanting American citizens. The principle then lies about like a loaded weapon ready for the hand of any authority that can bring forward a plausible claim of an urgent need.

The Japanese relocation program did not engage the First Amendment. In terms of freedom of speech and press, the society's record was far better in the second world war than in the first. There were a few prosecutions of German sympathizers, but not the mass hysteria that sent harmless men and women to prison for long terms. In World War I, Americans were prosecuted for objecting to the purchase of Liberty Bonds. In World War II, a test of patriotism was joining in the salute to the flag. Children were expelled from public school for refusing to do so; they were Jehovah's Witnesses who said their religion forbade such obeisance. In 1940, in *Minersville School District v. Gobitis*, the Supreme Court rejected an appeal by such children; only the chief justice, Harlan F. Stone, dissented. But the decision was widely criticized, and just three years later the Court changed its mind. A 6-to-3 majority in *West Virginia Board of Education v. Barnette* (1943) found that compelling the flag salute violated the First Amendment. Justice Jackson, writing for the majority, said:

> Compulsory unification of opinion achieves only the unanimity of the graveyard. It seems trite but necessary to say that the First Amendment to our Constitution was designed to avoid these ends by avoiding these beginnings. . . . We can have intellectual individualism and the rich cultural diversity that we owe to exceptional minds only at the price of occasional eccentricity and abnormal attitudes. When they are so harmless to others or to the State as those we deal with here, the price is not too great. But freedom to differ is not limited to things that do not matter much. That would be a mere shadow of freedom. The test of its substance is the right to differ as to things that touch the heart of the existing order.
>
> If there is any fixed star in our constitutional constellation, it is that no official, high or petty, can prescribe what shall be orthodox in politics, nationalism, religion or other matters of opinion or force citizens to confess by word or act their faith therein.

Justice Jackson's point that the First Amendment does not allow the state to compel speech was applied thirty-four years later by the Supreme Court to reverse the conviction of a Jehovah's Witness couple who had taped over the motto on New Hampshire license plates, "Live Free or Die." Chief Justice Warren E. Burger said that First Amendment freedom of thought "includes both the right to speak freely and the right to refrain from speaking at all."

At the end of World War II the First Amendment seemed to be in a strong position in the courts and in the country. The legal doctrines that had sent men and women to prison for years because they criticized the government or its officials were history. But within a few years the country was in the grip of another Red Scare. Fear ate away at freedom of speech and association. And the courts did not respond to the challenge in a timely and effective way.

The Cold War with the Soviet Union underlay the fear. Soviet imposition of Communist rule in Eastern European countries it had taken from German occupation by the end of the war—Poland, Czechoslovakia, and the rest—raised the specter of Soviet armies marching west. Germany itself, divided between East and West, was a source of particular tension. Inside the United States, ambitious politicians stoked the fear that disloyal Americans were helping the Communist cause. When Republicans won control of the House of Representatives in 1946, they used hearings of the House Committee on Un-American Activities to paint a disturbing picture of Communist infiltration into schools, universities, the press, and even Hollywood. Movie directors and writers were subpoenaed, and ten refused to testify—the Hollywood Ten. They were cited for contempt of Congress and prosecuted on that charge.

The unfriendly witnesses, as they were called, argued that forcing them to testify about their associations, and to name others, violated their freedom of speech and belief under the First Amendment. When that argument failed, some went to prison for contempt. Even those who avoided contempt citations were publicly humiliated and pictured as subversives. The Hollywood figures were blacklisted by the film industry. (Some wrote scripts under assumed names.) A magazine called *Red Channels* published lists of broadcast performers who it said were pro-Communist, and many were unable to appear on radio or television.

The Supreme Court considered the First Amendment issue in 1959 in *Barenblatt v. United States.* Lloyd Barenblatt, an instructor at Vassar College, had refused to tell the Un-American Activities Committee about past or present membership in the Communist Party. The Court rejected his constitutional arguments by a vote of 5 to 4. Justice Harlan, for the majority, said the interest of Congress in investigating subversive activity outweighed Barenblatt's interest in the privacy of his beliefs. He said the Court could not consider whether, as Barenblatt alleged, the committee was not interested in legislating but was engaged in exposure for exposure's sake. Justice Black, dissenting, said: "[The majority] leaves out the real interest in Barenblatt's silence, the interest of the people as a whole in being able to join organizations, advocate causes and make political 'mistakes' without later being subjected to governmental penalties for having dared to think for themselves. It is this right, the right to err politically, which keeps us strong as a nation."

There was one case in those years in which the Supreme Court found that a legislative investigation violated the First Amendment. The case arose from a curious procedure in New Hampshire that made the state attorney general a one-man investigating committee for the legislature. (New Hampshire at the time was dominated politically by the Far Right.) Paul Sweezy, a left-wing economics professor, refused to answer the attorney general's questions about a lecture he had given at the University of New Hampshire and about the Progressive Party, a left-wing third party. His contempt conviction was reversed by the Supreme Court by a vote of 6 to 3. The crucial opinion, focusing on the First Amendment, was a concurring opinion by Justice Frankfurter, joined by Justice Harlan—two who were the leading conservatives on the Court at the time. Justice Frankfurter weighed the competing interests as follows:

> The inviolability of privacy belonging to a citizen's political loyalty has so overwhelming an importance to the well-being of our kind of society that it cannot be constitutionally encroached upon on the basis of so meagre a countervailing interest of the State as may be argumentatively found in the remote, shadowy threat to the security of New Hampshire allegedly presented [by the Progressive Party]. ... When weighed against the grave harm resulting from governmental intrusion into the intellectual life of a university, justification

for compelling a witness to discuss the contents of his lecture appears grossly inadequate.

Frankfurter had been a professor at the Harvard Law School before being appointed to the Supreme Court by President Roosevelt in 1939. His defense of academic freedom in that opinion was often cited by embattled universities and their faculties in later years. The statement that the First Amendment protects academic life was also an answer, in its way, to the press's frequent (though unsuccessful) claim that it had a preferred position under the First Amendment.

But the Sweezy case stood alone for some years in granting First Amendment protection to a witness accused of Communist associations. Those who looked to the courts to stand against the political manipulation of fear were disappointed. Senate committees vied with the House Committee on Un-American Activities in exposing assertedly Red-tainted individuals. The Permanent Investigations Subcommittee became the most famous—or notorious, depending on one's view—when it was chaired by Senator Joe McCarthy. But the executive branch was equally important in the anti-Communist crusade of the late 1940s and 1950s.

President Harry S. Truman instituted a government-wide loyalty program that removed government employees found to be of doubtful loyalty because of supposed dangerous associations. Loyalty boards that passed these judgments acted on the basis of charges by informants whose names and testimony were often withheld from the accused. Efforts were made over many years to have the Supreme Court find that these methods, reminiscent of the denunciations that sent French victims to the guillotine in the years after the Revolution, denied the victims the due process of law guaranteed by the Constitution. But the efforts failed. The loyalty program and other anti-Communist measures by the Truman administration were a product of the Cold War and in part reflected genuine concern about Communist infiltration. But they were also an attempt to counter Republican charges that Democrats were "soft on communism," a political theme that reached its apogee in Senator McCarthy's talk of "twenty years of treason" dating back to Franklin Roosevelt's first inaugural in 1933.

Government employees suspected of disloyalty under the Truman program were offered hearings before special boards, but the hearings lacked essential elements of fair process. The charges were based on statements by unnamed informers who were not subject to cross-examination, and the charges themselves often wandered far afield from what could rationally be considered threats to government security. Dorothy Bailey, who had a nonsensitive federal job, was asked by a board member at her hearing, "Did you ever write a letter to the Red Cross about the segregation of blood?" Bailey was black, a graduate of Bryn Mawr. In volume 12 of the history of the Supreme Court being written and published with funds left to the United States by Justice Holmes, William M. Wiecek relates that episode and observes: "The prevalent racism and sexism of the era infected the security screening process, and some investigators hoped to root out civil rights activists and civil libertarians."

Dorothy Bailey was denied permanent federal employment because "reasonable grounds exist for belief that you are disloyal. . . . " She sued, challenging the denial of a right to confront her accusers. The United States Court of Appeals for the District of Columbia Circuit ruled against her by a vote of 2 to 1. The Supreme Court divided equally, 4–4, one justice not sitting; that had the effect of upholding the Court of Appeals decision. The Supreme Court never did squarely resolve the troubling issue of the use of unnamed informants in loyalty-security proceedings.

The great legal test of the period came in the Truman administration's prosecution of leaders of the Communist Party, which ended in the Supreme Court's 1951 decision in *Dennis v. United States.* Eleven defendants were charged with conspiring to "teach and advocate the overthrow and destruction of the Government of the United States by force and violence." They were not charged with actually attempting the overthrow, or with conspiring to do so, but only with conspiring to advocate it—a distinction often lost in the theatrics that surrounded the trial. The party's own documents abjured the use of violence, but former party members who testified for the prosecution said that these professions of support for peaceful change were "Aesopian language" concealing violent intentions. The jury convicted the eleven.

The United States Court of Appeals for the Second Circuit affirmed the conviction in an opinion by that most respected judge, Learned Hand. He offered a new formula for Holmes's clear and present danger test: "whether the gravity of the 'evil,' discounted by its improbability, justifies such invasion of free speech as is necessary to avoid the danger." If the perceived danger is very great, then, repression is allowable even if there is only a minimal chance of the danger actually occurring. This sliding scale was adopted by Chief Justice Fred M. Vinson in the Supreme Court, and the convictions were upheld.

The niceties of legal doctrine could not conceal what was really happening in *Dennis*. In the world, the Soviet Union presented profound dangers. In the United States, the open Communist Party presented no threat to the American system of government. What was a threat was the spy network maintained by the Soviet Union. The extent of this espionage effort was disclosed by the publication in 1995 of what were called the Venona documents, cables from Soviet agents intercepted and decrypted by the United States. They showed that the USSR used American Communists and secret supporters intensely to try to obtain security information. But U.S. officials, knowing the Venona findings contemporaneously, chose not to prosecute Communist leaders for conducting or supporting espionage but instead to charge them, in *Dennis*, with conspiring to teach and advocate the necessity of revolutionary violence. Why? Professor Martin H. Redish of Northwestern University Law School wrote, convincingly to me, that a possible explanation was the intended goal of FBI Director J. Edgar Hoover: to send the message to the country, "Engage in unpopular political thought at your own risk." In short, the decision to prosecute Dennis and the others for teaching and advocacy was political in origin and consequence.

Moreover, there was a deep irony in the legal legacy of the case, Judge Hand's reformulation of the clear and present danger test. Hand had never liked the test or considered it a wise reading of the First Amendment. He said of Justice Holmes's authorship of it, "For once, Homer nodded." During World War I, as a federal trial judge, Hand had proposed a different approach when the radical magazine *The Masses* challenged an order by Postmaster General Burleson barring it from the mails. Hand thought the crucial question should be whether the speech or writing that led to the government action was expressly intended to bring about an unlawful result. But his approach was rejected on appeal at the time and was forgotten by the time of the *Dennis* case. Hand felt obliged to follow the Holmes approach, though his version of it was much weaker than what was intended by Holmes—who would have protected intentional appeals to lawlessness if they had no immediate danger of succeeding. Personally, Hand took a dim view of the *Dennis* prosecution. He wrote a friend, "Personally I should never have prosecuted those birds."

Justices Black and Douglas dissented in the Supreme Court. Black wrote: "Public opinion being what it is now, few will protest the conviction of these Communist petitioners. There is hope, however, that in calmer times, when present pressures, passions and fears subside, this or some later Court will restore the First Amendment liberties to the high preferred place where they belong in a free society."

Freedom of speech and belief was seriously damaged during the second Red Scare. The congressional hearings, the

Dennis prosecution, the federal loyalty program, and numerous other state and federal anti-Communist laws encouraged all but the bravest Americans to stick to conformist views. The First Amendment, which from 1930 to 1943 (when the *Barnette* flag-salute case was decided) had been interpreted ever more broadly by the Supreme Court, was left in a shrunken state. The Court had shown that it was not inclined to stand against what Justice Black called popular "passions and fears."

But in time the situation changed, in the country and the Court. The public's support for Red-hunting ebbed with the disgrace and death of Senator McCarthy after he was condemned by the Senate in 1954. In 1957, in *Yates v. United States*, the Supreme Court in an opinion by Justice Harlan read the law as prohibiting advocacy of violent overthrow only when it was accompanied by an effort at action to that end, not mere abstract advocacy.

The law that prohibited advocacy of violent overthrow, the Smith Act, also made it criminal to be a member of a party with such a program. In order to sustain the membership clause's constitutionality, the government prosecuted Communists who it said were "active" members. (A Justice Department lawyer ironically explained to me at the time, off the record: "It's not enough to be a member of the party; you have to be a"—raising his voice—"*member.*") On that basis, the Supreme Court by a 5–4 vote affirmed the conviction of Junius Scales, a Communist in North Carolina. A Columbia Law School professor who had been a war crimes prosecutor at Nuremberg, Telford Taylor, asked the Kennedy administration to commute Scales's five-year sentence. Despite fears of a political backlash, Attorney General Robert Kennedy recommended the commutation and President Kennedy granted it. Scales was the last Smith Act prisoner.

In 1969 the Supreme Court adopted a new test for advocacy of violent or unlawful action. In *Brandenburg v. Ohio* a Ku Klux Klan leader had denounced blacks and Jews at a rally. The Court reversed his conviction. To pass constitutional muster, it said, a conviction must be for advocacy (1) directed to "inciting or producing imminent lawless action," and (2) "likely to produce such action." The first element, the speaker's intent, followed Judge Hand's approach. The second, and the word "imminent," incorporated Justice Holmes's. The *Dennis* conviction would not have passed the test.

The calmer times for which Justice Black had hoped had evidently arrived, and the First Amendment was restored to its high position. The Supreme Court proceeded to hold a number of anti-Communist laws unconstitutional. An especially interesting case was *Lamont v. Postmaster General*, decided in 1965. As the Cold War intensified, the government adopted a program to discourage Americans from receiving Soviet publications such as *Pravda*. When a copy arrived at the post office, officials would send a notice to the addressee with a postcard that he could return saying that he wanted the "Communist political propaganda" to be delivered to him. The Kennedy administration abolished the practice—whereupon Congress, under pressure from anti-Communist zealots, wrote it into a statute. Many of the addressees were libraries, which could brave the stigma of saying they wanted

"Communist political propaganda." One individual subscriber, Corliss Lamont, challenged the law in court. The Supreme Court held it unconstitutional. Justice Douglas said requiring return of the postcard "is almost certain to have a deterrent effect. . . . Public officials, like school teachers who have no tenure, might think they would invite disaster if they read what the Federal Government says contains the seeds of treason." The Lamont decision, surprisingly, was the first that ever found a federal law in violation of the First Amendment.

The times did not remain calm. Not long after the *Lamont* decision the country was bitterly, savagely divided over the Vietnam War. The 1968 Democratic Convention in Chicago saw street battles between antiwar protesters and squads of police who brutally attacked the protesters. President Lyndon Johnson privately fulminated against his critics, saying that such eminent newspaper columnists as Walter Lippmann and James B. Reston were dupes of communism. But he did not use the federal prosecutorial power, as President Wilson had, for widespread attempts to suppress political disagreement. There were some prosecutions, notably of the antiwar group that came to be known as the Chicago Seven. Their case turned into a shouting match with an irascible, antagonistic judge, Julius Hoffman. In the end, all convictions resulting from that trial were overturned on appeal.

Divisions if anything deepened after the election of Richard M. Nixon as president in 1968. Leading universities were disrupted by student protests; Nixon referred to the protesters as "these bums." Speaking to the nation from the White House on April 30, 1970, Nixon said he was widening the war into Cambodia lest the United States be seen in the world as "a pitiful helpless giant." A few days later, at Kent State University in Ohio, national guardsmen fired their rifles at a group of unarmed students, killing four.

The Supreme Court's response to the Vietnam turmoil was utterly different from the Court's submission to the Wilson administration's prosecutions in 1919. The signal decision was in *Bond v. Floyd* in 1966. Julian Bond was elected to the Georgia House of Representatives, but the House voted to exclude him on the ground that he could not honestly swear—as required of members—to support the Georgia and federal constitutions. Bond, a significant black figure in the civil rights movement, had endorsed a statement by the movement's Student Nonviolent Coordinating Committee. It said, "We are in sympathy with, and support, the men in this country who are unwilling to respond to a military draft."

Bond explained to a Georgia legislative committee that he was not urging people to break laws but was simply trying "to say that I admired the courage of someone who could act on his convictions knowing that he faces pretty stiff consequences." The Supreme Court held unanimously that exclusion of Bond from the legislature violated the First Amendment. Chief Justice Warren's opinion said it needed no discussion to show that Bond could not, constitutionally, have been convicted of a crime for his statements. Eugene Debs, the Socialist Party leader, had been convicted in World War I and sentenced to ten years in prison for making very similar comments about the draft—and in 1919 the Supreme Court unanimously upheld his conviction.

Eugene Debs was pardoned by President Warren G. Harding in 1921. In 1920, Congress repealed the Sedition Act of 1918. In 1976, President Gerald Ford said the day the Japanese-Americans were removed from the West Coast in 1944 was "a sad day in American history"; in 1988, Congress passed and President Ronald Reagan signed an act giving modest compensation to survivors of the 1944 relocation program and saying that it had been motivated largely by "racial prejudice, wartime hysteria and a failure of political leadership."

Repeatedly, then, times of fear and stress were followed, some years after the fear ebbed, by regret and apology. But that pattern was challenged by the first episode of fear in the twenty-first century: the great national fear of terrorism after the attacks of September 11, 2001, on the World Trade Center and the Pentagon. President George W. Bush used that fear to adopt a series of programs that broke sharply with American law. He authorized the use of torture and other harsh methods of interrogation on suspected terrorists detained in a prison at Guantanamo Bay, Cuba, and elsewhere in secret CIA prisons. (Such treatment was in violation of the Geneva Conventions—treaties to which the United States was a party—and of a federal criminal statute.) He ordered wiretapping of Americans' international telephone calls, in violation of a criminal law. He detained American citizens suspected of terrorist ties indefinitely, without trial or access to counsel.

The war on terror, as President Bush called it, differed from the past times of war and fear in its endless quality. It was hard to envisage a point of victory when the world's terrorists would surrender: hard to imagine the most-publicized terrorist leader, Osama bin Laden, boarding an American ship to surrender as Japanese leaders did at the end of World War II. So it was difficult to see when a time might come for regret and apology for the cruel excesses of the war on terror.

Measures such as indefinite detention and torture did not engage the First Amendment. They were reminders that the freedoms of speech and of the press are not the only tests of a humane and free society. Freedom from arbitrary arrest, detention, and physical abuse is just as crucial. The central concern among the Framers of the American Constitution was concentrated power, and the checks and balances they built into our system of government were intended to prevent that kind of power. The aim of the Bush measures was to give the president precisely what the Framers had wanted to avoid: unilateral power unchecked by the other branches of government—and unchecked by the press. The Bush administration worked to exclude press scrutiny—and hence public accountability—by the most sweeping secrecy in American history. Even documents that had long been public were recalled and classified. Journalists who succeeded in exposing secret measures like the wiretapping order were threatened with prosecution for espionage.

Even in a country with constitutional guarantees of freedom, something more is needed to resist fear and its manipulators. That is courage. And there have been men and women of courage, lawyers and journalists and citizens, in all of America's crises. Two were in Montana in World War I, and they will serve as examples: Burton K. Wheeler, the

United States district attorney for the state (famous later as an isolationist senator before World War II), and the single federal district judge for Montana, George M. Bourquin. As described in Clemens Work's book, Wheeler persuaded a grand jury not to indict forty-eight Montanans brought in on sedition complaints in 1918. (The grand jurors had to be courageous, too, because their names were published.) Wheeler drafted a statement that the grand jury issued: "In many cases . . . it has been found by us that reports of so-called "seditious utterances" and "disloyal statements" were highly colored and greatly exaggerated. . . . The testimony disclosed complaints of words of a most trivial character showing a specie of hysteria prevalent in the minds of people in many communities. . . . "

Thanks to Wheeler, and to Judge Bourquin, there were no successful Espionage Act prosecutions in Montana. Judge Bourquin heard a petition for habeas corpus from a man who had been convicted of sedition under the state law for refusing to kiss the American flag. Bourquin decided that a federal judge could not intervene, but he wrote:

> Like religion, patriotism is a virtue so indispensable and exalted, its excesses pass with little censure. But when . . . it descends to fanaticism, it is of the reprehensible quality of the religion that incited the massacre of St. Bartholomew, the tortures of the Inquisition, the fires of Smithfield, the scaffolds of Salem, and is equally cruel and murderous. In its name, as in that of Liberty, what crimes have been committed! In every age it, too, furnishes its heresy hunters and its

witch burners, and it, too, is a favorite mask for hypocrisy, assuming a virtue which it haveth not.

I wonder whether Justice Robert H. Jackson was aware of Judge Bourquin's words when he wrote, decades later, in a case about a woman who was supposedly a risk to American security, Ellen Knauff: "Security is like liberty, in that many are the crimes committed in its name."

8

"Another's Lyric"

On February 22, 1971, in the Supreme Court chamber, Professor Melville B. Nimmer of the Law School of the University of California at Los Angeles rose to argue in the case of *Paul Robert Cohen v. California.* Before he could say a word, Chief Justice Warren E. Burger addressed him. "The Court is thoroughly familiar with the factual setting of this case," he said, "and it will not be necessary for you, I'm sure, to dwell on the facts." Nimmer said he would keep his statement of the facts brief. His client had been convicted of "engaging in tumultuous conduct," he said. "What this young man did was to walk through a courthouse corridor in Los Angeles County . . . wearing a jacket on which were inscribed the words 'Fuck the Draft.'"

Those were of course the words that Chief Justice Burger did not want to hear in the courtroom. (He may have been particularly sensitive because a group of nuns were there that day.) But Nimmer understood that to shy away from the words was in a sense to give his case away. He was courageous, he was wise, and he won the case. By a vote of 5 to 4, the Supreme Court reversed

Cohen's conviction, holding that it violated his right to free expression under the First Amendment.

Justice John Marshall Harlan, writing the opinion of the court, made of this trivial incident a luminous statement on freedom of expression. "One man's vulgarity is another's lyric," he said. In the context of the Vietnam War, the "unseemly expletive" Cohen used was a form of political protest. Justice Harlan went on:

> The constitutional right of free expression is powerful medicine in a society as diverse and populous as ours. It is designed and intended to remove governmental restraints from the arena of public discussion, putting the decision as to what views shall be voiced largely into the hands of each of us, in the hope that use of such freedom will ultimately produce a more capable citizenry and more perfect polity and in the belief that no other approach would comport with the premise of individual dignity and choice upon which our political system rests. . . . That the air may at times seem filled with verbal cacophony is, in this sense, not a sign of weakness but of strength.

Justice Harlan emphasized the political in his analysis of Cohen's use of the expletive. But it was sexual offensiveness that got Cohen arrested, and official disapproval of sexual content was a staple element in American legal conflict for many decades.

In the early years of the twentieth century such serious literary works as D.H. Lawrence's *Lady Chatterly's Lover* and

Theodore Dreiser's *An American Tragedy* were banned as obscene. Judges found a work obscene if any passage in it might have an unfortunate effect on susceptible readers, such as children. Then, in 1933, U.S. Customs seized a copy of the French edition of James Joyce's *Ulysses* as it was brought into the country. The novel, now generally considered a masterpiece, had been banned since 1920 when the New York Society for the Suppression of Vice complained about an episode in which Joyce's leading character, Leopold Bloom, masturbated. But after a trial over the customs seizure, Federal District Judge John M. Woolsey found that *Ulysses* was not obscene. He used a new test, judging a work by the effect of its dominant theme on an average reader. This more permissive standard—we might say more grownup—was widely adopted.

In 1948 what was widely expected to be an important test case reached the Supreme Court. It was a ban on *Memoirs of Hecate County*, a novel by the eminent literary critic Edmund Wilson. (The objection was apparently to a passage about a woman's orgasm.) But one justice did not sit, and the Court then divided equally, 4 to 4. That was probably the last time the Supreme Court allowed a ban on a serious book to stand.

The Court's first broad pronouncement on censorship of the supposedly obscene came in 1957, in *Roth v. United States*. Sam Roth had been convicted of mailing an obscene publication in violation of a federal law. The Supreme Court affirmed the conviction. But the opinion seemed to look both ways, taking obscenity outside the protection of the First Amendment but defining it narrowly. Justice Brennan said that anything with "even the slightest redeeming social importance—unorthodox ideas, controversial ideas, even ideas hateful to the prevailing climate of opinion" was protected by the First Amendment. But history, he said, showed that obscenity had been treated as "utterly without redeeming social importance." In 1792, thirteen of the fourteen states that had ratified the Constitution provided for the prosecution of libel—and made "either blasphemy or profanity, or both, statutory crimes." So it was "apparent," Justice Brennan said, that obscenity, like libel, was "outside the protection intended for speech and press." (It was unusual for Justice Brennan, who was anything but an originalist in interpreting the Constitution, to rely on such history. And just seven years later, in *New York Times v. Sullivan*, he ended the historic exclusion of libel from the amendment's protection.)

"However," Justice Brennan went on, "sex and obscenity are not synonymous. . . . The portrayal of sex, e.g. in art, literature and scientific works, is not itself sufficient reason to deny material the constitutional protection of freedom of speech and press. Sex, a great and mysterious motive in human life, has indisputably been a subject of absorbing interest to mankind through the ages; it is one of the vital problems of human interest and public concern." So Justice Brennan propounded this test of what is censorable: "whether to the average person, applying contemporary community standards, the dominant theme of the material taken as a whole appeals to the prurient interest."

Justices Douglas and Black dissented, hewing to their position that the First Amendment ordains absolute freedom.

Justice Douglas's opinion said the amendment was intended to "preclude courts as well as legislatures from weighing the values of speech against silence." Douglas said he had "the same confidence in the ability of our people to reject noxious literature as I have in their capacity to sort out the true from the false in theology, economics, politics or any other field."

Movies engaged the Supreme Court as much as books. For a long time films were thought to be outside constitutional protection. But in 1952 the Court ended that assumption. In *Burstyn v. Wilson* it set aside a New York ban on a movie called *The Miracle* that had been found contemptuous of Christian religion. The Court said such thematic censorship was unconstitutional; Justice Tom C. Clark put it that the state had "no legitimate interest in protecting all or any religions from views distasteful to them. . . . "

Censorship of films with controversial themes was one thing. Provocative sexual scenes were quite another, and tortuously difficult for the Supreme Court to handle. The test for obscenity laid down by the *Roth* case was hardly self-executing. Judges, like everyone else, disagreed on whether particular films "appealed to the prurient interest" and on what "contemporary community standards" were. For a period of years the Supreme Court dealt with the problem by actually viewing the films at issue in a screening room set up in the court building. Justices Black and Douglas never came; they thought nothing could be banned. The other justices did. Justice Harlan, whose eyesight by then was severely impaired, brought a law clerk with him to tell him what was going on.

The result was chaos. In case after case the Supreme Court simply issued a brief order reversing or upholding a ban, with little or no explanation of how it came to that conclusion. In others, various justices issued conflicting opinions with no majority view emerging. In 1964, in *Jacobellis v. Ohio*, Justice Stewart offered, for himself, a much-quoted pronouncement, saying that criminal antiobscenity laws could be applied constitutionally only to "hard-core pornography." He doubted that he could intelligibly define what that was, Justice Stewart said; "but I know it when I see it, and the motion picture involved in this case is not that." Justice Brennan added a further element to the test he laid down in the *Roth* case: that, to be bannable, material must be "utterly without redeeming social value." A majority of the Court withdrew that requirement in 1973, giving local communities greater rights to define, and ban, obscenity. Justice Brennan, dissenting, said he had come to the view that his attempt to lay down a standard in *Roth* had not worked. He would abandon all restraints on alleged obscenity, he said, except those imposed to protect children and to prevent "unconsenting adults" from having pornography thrust upon them.

In those years the Court acted like a national film licensing board. It was a hopeless task, performed clumsily. Some critics argued that it was not only a daunting notion but one outside the proper scope of the First Amendment. Professor Robert H. Bork of the Yale Law School said the amendment's protection of speech and press should be limited to political expression. "There is no basis," he said, "for judicial intervention to protect any other form of expression, be it scientific, literary or that variety of expression we call obscene or pornographic." To go be-

yond the explicitly political, Bork argued, was to involve courts
in value judgments that should be left to the political process.
He also argued, in disagreement with Holmes and Brandeis
and the whole course of constitutional interpretation since
1930, that the First Amendment should not protect advocacy of
law violation or overthrow of the government. (Bork became a
judge, was nominated to the Supreme Court by President Reagan, and rejected by the Senate.)

On the particular issue of protecting sexual expression,
critics made a number of arguments. One was that allowing
pornography made for a coarser society. Bork suggested that
it caused a "pollution of the moral and aesthetic atmosphere
precisely analogous to smoke pollution," altering "attitudes
toward love and sex . . . and views of social institutions such as
marriage and the family.".

Perhaps reflecting the idea that pornography can be a form
of pollution, or perhaps in accordance with Justice Brennan's
concern about unconsenting adults having it thrust upon
them, a number of cities limited the locations where adult
theaters could operate. In 1986, by a vote of 5 to 4, the
Supreme Court upheld a local zoning law providing, among
other things, that such a theater could not be located within
500 feet of a residential area. Television and radio broadcasting, regulated by the Federal Communications Commission
(FCC), has been seen by the Court as posing a danger of offending unconsenting listeners and viewers. In 1978 the
Court upheld an FCC finding that a radio station had violated
the law by broadcasting a monologue by the comedian
George Carlin on "seven dirty words."

Another argument against constitutional protection for pornography, made by a leading feminist law professor, Catherine MacKinnon, was that it was a way of subordinating women. The city of Indianapolis adopted an ordinance criminalizing pornography on that basis, but the United States Court of Appeals for the Seventh Circuit held it unconstitutional. In 1986 a commission appointed by President Reagan's attorney general, Edwin L. Meese, found that sexually violent material could cause antisocial conduct and that "degrading" material could "increase acceptance of the proposition that women like to be forced into sexual practices." The data offered by the commission were widely questioned.

There are powerful reasons to disagree with the critics and support constitutional protection for artistic, literary, and scientific expression, including the sexual. Zealots have made their mark in American history with censorship of all kinds. Politicians often find it easier to play to what H.L. Mencken, that coruscating critic of American foolishness, called the "booboisie." Independent judges like John M. Woolsey can stand against the mob that wants to ban a *Ulysses*, usually without having read it. The Supreme Court is well-placed to counter local pressure groups that have persuaded politicians to ban a film like *The Miracle*. A national, constitutional forum has its value. The expression that opens the minds of a people is not limited to the political.

Moreover, sex and politics can be intermingled. That was true in *Cohen v. California*. And it was true in a case that came before the Supreme Court in 1988, *Hustler v. Falwell*. Its facts made Paul Robert Cohen's rude jacket look like a Sunday school lesson. Campari, the aperitif, had run a series of magazine advertisements labeled "the first time"—the first time those portrayed had tasted Campari but, by innuendo, their first sexual encounter. *Hustler* magazine ran what it called a "parody advertisement" saying that the Reverend Jerry Falwell's "first time" was with his mother in an outhouse. Falwell sued for libel and intentional infliction of emotional distress. A jury rejected the libel claim, reasoning that the ad could not be taken as fact, but awarded $150,000 for emotional distress.

In the Supreme Court, a brief as friend of the court was filed by the Association of American Editorial Cartoonists. It consisted of political cartoons from American history, starting with one that showed George Washington as an ass and including the famous Thomas Nast cartoons of Boss Tweed and his Tammany Hall political gang as vultures. At the argument—an extraordinary one—the justices repeatedly referred to the cartoons. At one point, counsel for *Hustler* said the George Washington example showed that in the open American society even revered leaders had been subjected to vicious lampooning. Justice Scalia responded that he thought "old George" could stand that, "but with your mother in an outhouse?" The Court unanimously set aside Falwell's damage judgment. The opinion, by Chief Justice William H. Rehnquist, relied on the libel decision in *New York Times v. Sullivan.* Even when couched as a claimed deliberate infliction of emotional distress, Chief Justice Rehnquist said, a suit for damage to a public figure's *amour propre* could not succeed unless he or she proved that what was said was deliberately or recklessly false—and a lampoon could not be factually false.

Americans today would find it hard to believe what was suppressed in the past, and not only the distant past. In 1956 a San Francisco bookseller, Lawrence Ferlinghetti, was prosecuted for selling Allen Ginsberg's poem "Howl." A municipal judge, Clayton W. Horn, ended that repressive folly. "The best method of censorship is by the people," he said, "as self-guardians of public opinion, and not by the government."

As to suppression of pornography on film, in the end courts became irrelevant. Technology and public opinion overtook all the legal logic-chopping. By the end of the twentieth century, millions of Americans were watching, on their computers or on cable television, what Justice Stewart would have described as hard-core pornography. The Federal Communications Commission stuck doggedly to its role as nanny, imposing heavy fines on broadcasters who televised the 2004 Superbowl game in which Janet Jackson, in a halftime show, unexpectedly exposed a breast. But most Americans probably couldn't care less.

Or most people in other Western societies. Britain, for example, was long regarded as a straitlaced country. For centuries, plays had to be submitted to the Lord Chamberlain for approval before they were produced; he blue-penciled anything suggestive or disrespectful of authority. Parliament abolished that requirement in 1968. And the top-selling tabloid in Britain (and the world), Rupert Murdoch's *Sun*, publishes every day a photograph of a topless model with much more of a come-hither look than Janet Jackson.

The critics' objections may be futile now, but they are right to worry about the flood of pornography and the general coarsening of our societies. There is a difference between *Ulysses* and adult movies, so called. When literature no longer has room for subtle intimations of love and sex—no room, say, for Jane Austen—we are the losers. But the bluenoses who kept Americans from reading Joyce and Lawrence made censorship intellectually unacceptable, and attempts to draw a line somewhere else—by judges and politicians— did not work.

9

"Vagabonds and Outlaws"

In Dickens's *Martin Chuzzlewit*, the eponymous hero sails to America on a packet boat. In New York harbor it is boarded by newsboys who cry out the latest in their papers—the *New York Stabber*, the *Peeper*, the *Family Spy* and so on. "Here's the Sewer!" shouts one. "Here's the Sewer's exposure of the Wall Street Gang, and the Sewer's exposure of the Washington gang, and the Sewer's exclusive account of a flagrant act of dishonesty committed by the Secretary of State when he was eight years old; now communicated, at a great expense, by his own nurse."

The nineteenth-century American press could certainly be, well, piquant. But the odd thing is that a century later American newspapers had moved toward respectability, while the British press could be almost beyond Dickensian parody in the extravagance of its make-believe.

In 1982 an unemployed Englishman, Michael Fagan, got into Buckingham Palace one night and made his way into the Queen's bedroom, where he had a chat with her. The *Sunday People*, a weekly, said it had polled its readers on what should be done, and the answer was that the Queen and Prince Philip should share a double bed. The story ran on page one under the headline, "Give Her a Cuddle, Philip."

My favorite example of British tabloid style began on February 25, 1987, when *The Sun* published a story with this lead: "Elton John is at the center of a shocking drugs and vice scandal involving teen-age 'rent boys', The Sun can reveal today." "Rent boy" is British journalese for male prostitute. The story said its source was one "Graham X." The next day's *Sun* relied on Graham X for a story saying, "Kinky superstar Elton John loved to snort cocaine through rolled-up $100 bills." John denied both stories and brought two libel actions against *The Sun*. Over the following months, there were many more stories, each followed by a libel writ. The last was headlined "Mystery of Elton's Silent Dogs." John, it said, had had his "vicious Rottweiler dogs" silenced by a "horrific operation." John sued again: his seventeenth libel action since the start of *The Sun*'s campaign.

For some reason, possibly the English fondness for dogs, the last of the suits was scheduled for trial first: on December 12, 1988. That morning, *The Sun*'s banner headline was "Sorry Elton." *The Sun* had settled the seventeen lawsuits by paying John 1 million pounds in damages and about half as much again for his legal fees. "We are delighted that The Sun and Elton have become friends again," the paper said, "and we are sorry that we were lied to by a teenager living in a world of fantasy." The "apology" was for the boy's lies, not for the editors' credulousness or, more likely, coaching.

British editors and reporters stayed longer than their American counterparts with the old model of their trade: raffish, disrespectful. But the classic portrayal of the old style was American: the 1930s stage comedy *The Front Page* and its movie version, *Our Gal Friday*. Reporters sat around the press room drinking whiskey out of paper cups and trading lies. The hero hid an escaped criminal in a rolltop desk. The demon editor demanded that the exclusive story have the paper's name in the lead paragraph (like the first of *The Sun*'s fictions about Elton John). They were ruffian reporters, street-smart but without intellectual or social pretensions.

In the mid–twentieth century, American reporters began drinking white wine. They had college, some even graduate degrees. And their ambitions climbed. They wanted to be in Washington, the center of the world. They wanted to go to dinner parties with the secretary of state. That is a bit of a caricature, but not much. Reporters used to be outsiders, badly paid. Now they, at any rate those in Washington and others among the top in the profession, are part of the establishment, upper-middle class in outlook. They call themselves journalists instead of reporters. There is a danger in all that: the danger of becoming too close to power. It is a palpable danger in Washington. Writing critically about a cabinet member is hard after sitting next to his or her spouse at a dinner party.

A notable British columnist, Bernard Levin of *The Times* of London, warned tellingly against the press's assuming "responsibility"—using that word in an English sense of commitment to official institutions. "The press," he wrote, "has no duty to be responsible at all, and it will be an ill day for freedom if it should ever acquire one. ... We are and must remain vagabonds and outlaws, for only by so remaining shall we be able to keep the faith by which we live, which is the pursuit of knowledge that others would like unpursued and the making of comments that others would prefer unmade." (Levin loved champagne and opera, as it happened, but that did not stop him from scourging the mighty when they went wrong.)

The highest duty of the press—to inform the public about its governors—was defined in the earliest days of the United States by James Madison. In a republic, he said, the people are the ultimate sovereigns; they depend for their information on the press, which must therefore be free to "canvass the merits and measures of public men." Madison was something of a romantic about the press. He wrote in 1799: "To the press alone, chequered as it is with abuses, the world is indebted for all the triumphs which have been gained by reason and humanity over error and oppression."

The American press has to perform its Madisonian function today in relation to a federal government that Madison could scarcely have imagined. It was tiny in his day, and it remained modest in size and role until Franklin Roosevelt's New Deal in the 1930s; as New Deal programs went into effect, new governmental agencies were born and the government in Washington began to assume responsibilities that had formerly been exercised by the states or by no government. Now the federal government is huge and powerful. Its officials often operate in secret, and they are protected by armies of spokesmen. A government that George Washington warned to avoid foreign entanglements is entangled politically and militarily around the world.

Coping with a government of that character requires press institutions with large resources. The raggle-taggle newspapers of the eighteenth century could not have coped with the Pentagon, and neither can their contemporary equivalent, bloggers. It took a newspaper as established as the *Washington Post* to carry off the investigation of Watergate, and as the *New York Times* to publish the Pentagon Papers. Each of those episodes required, as well, proprietors of courage in the face of economic and legal threats: Katharine Graham of the *Post* and Arthur Ochs Sulzberger of the *Times*.

In his opinion in the Pentagon Papers case, Justice Stewart said the role of the press was especially important in matters of national security. In that area, he said, the usual legislative and judicial checks and balances on executive power scarcely operate; Congress and the courts tend to defer to the president. So, he wrote, "the only effective restraint upon executive policy and power . . . may lie in an enlightened citizenry—in an informed and critical public opinion. For this reason, it is perhaps here that a press that is alert, aware and free most vitally serves the purpose of the First Amendment. For without an informed and free press there cannot be an enlightened people."

To Justice Stewart's adjectives—informed, free, alert, aware—must be added courageous. By those standards, the American press failed sadly when it met its next great test after Vietnam: the government's policy and power after the terrorist attacks on New York and Washington on September 11, 2001.

Within a few months of those attacks President George W. Bush claimed the power to detain any American citizen as an enemy combatant and hold him or her indefinitely, without trial or access to counsel. His attorney general ordered thousands of aliens swept up and held for months on suspicion, often humiliated and physically abused. (Not one was convicted of an offense related to terrorism.)

President Bush and his aides set about preparing the way for a war on Iraq by trying to persuade the American public that the Iraqi regime of Saddam Hussein had been involved in the September 11 terrorist attacks. Their propaganda campaign was extraordinarily successful. By March 2003, just before the war was launched, polls showed that 45 percent of Americans believed Saddam Hussein was "personally involved" in the September 11 attacks, and 44 percent said that some of the men who hijacked planes that day were Iraqis. Both beliefs were untrue, indeed preposterous. So much for the "enlightened citizenry" that Justice Stewart said was essential.

Where was the press in that period? The kindest answer would be: out to lunch. When the government seized two American citizens and detained them without trial as "enemy combatants," there were brief newspaper stories—with no sense of the constitutional stakes. The sweep of aliens got little attention until it was long over. The march toward war in Iraq had so little scrutiny that both the *Washington Post* and the *New York Times* later apologized for their failure. When a protest march took place in Washington before the Iraq invasion, a story in the *Post* mocked the demonstrators as "dudes" and "Patchouli girls."

Watergate and Vietnam had seemed to signal a new attitude on the part of what could be called the establishment press. In the years after World War II, it had treated federal officials with deferential respect. The leading correspondents and columnists shared the government's viewpoint on the commanding issue of the day, the contest with the Soviet Union. They credited officials with good faith and superior knowledge. Those assumptions collapsed in the Vietnam War. Correspondents there reported the situation far more accurately than official statements, and high officials engaged in deliberate deception.

Professors Harold Edgar and Benno Schmidt Jr. of the Columbia Law School wrote afterward that the *Times*'s decision to publish the Pentagon Papers symbolized "the passing of an era in which newsmen could be counted upon to work within reasonably well understood boundaries in disclosing information that politicians deemed sensitive." There had been a "symbiotic relationship between politicians and the press," they said, but now the press "intended to become an adversary."

What happened to those brave words after September 11? Instead of acting as a critic, or even a skeptic, the press performed more like a stenographer for official views. It printed President Bush's statements about his "war on terror" without paying particular note to the extraordinary power he was asserting. It hardly raised an eyebrow when the attorney general, John Ashcroft, told a Senate hearing: "To those who scare peace-loving people with phantoms of lost liberty, my message is this: Your tactics only aid terrorists, for they erode our national unity and diminish our resolve. They give ammunition to America's enemies."

Why was the press so submissive after 9/11? One reason was that, like the American public generally, editors were stunned by the terrorist attacks and felt the need for national unity against the perpetrators. That meant, for most, uniting behind the president. Moreover, to criticize the president in the atmosphere of fear could seem unpatriotic. Indeed, Attorney General Ashcroft had said that disagreement was unpatriotic. The sense of intimidation came also from the extreme right-wing voices on radio and television talk shows, one of whom said she regretted that the offices of the *New York Times* had not been bombed.

The extent of press submissiveness to the White House was demonstrated by broadcasters a month after 9/11. When five major television networks broadcast a taped message by Osama bin Laden, the terrorist leader, President Bush's national security adviser, Condoleezza Rice, got top executives of the networks on a conference telephone call. She urged them to eliminate "inflammatory language" from any future bin Laden tapes they used. She also warned that his talks might include coded instructions to terrorists—a singularly unpersuasive point, since his tapes had first been broadcast on an Arabic-language network. The American network executives agreed to broadcast only short segments of any future tapes. One of them said, "We're not going to step on the landmines she [Rice] was talking about." A more candid statement would have been, "We don't want to look unpatriotic."

In time, the press began to recover from its fear and lassitude. The brazen character of President Bush's claims of unilateral power became increasingly hard to overlook. One of his Justice Department lawyers advised him that he could order the torture of alleged terrorist detainees, and that Congress was without power to stop him. As a result of that legal opinion, dozens of foreign detainees were tortured, and some killed. Pictures of tortured men in Abu Ghraib prison in Iraq shocked the country.

The end of the deferential time was signaled by the decision of the *New York Times* to publish a story disclosing that President Bush had secretly ordered wiretapping of Americans' international telephone calls without obtaining the warrants required by law. The order was an explicit violation of a federal criminal statute. Once again, as in the legal memorandum claiming a presidential power to order torture, the assertion was that the president was above the law. That was the exact opposite of what was thought to be the lesson of Watergate: that the law applied to the high as to the low. The press could not, and did not, miss the growing evidence of abuse of power. Right-wing voices accused the *Times* of "treason" for publishing the story about warrantless wiretapping, and the reporters who wrote it were threatened with subpoenas for their sources. But the paper stood its ground, and the reporters won the Pulitzer Prize.

Because I spent years in England, I find informative the difference between British and American attitudes toward press freedom. In 1981 a civil-liberties organization brought suit on behalf of a prisoner who said he had been mistreated in a British jail. The prisoner's lawyer, Harriet Harman, asked for documents on the prison rules. The government objected, but the trial judge ordered that some of them be given to Harman. She read them out in open court. A newspaper reporter, uncertain of his shorthand, asked her for a copy. She gave it to him—and for that was convicted of contempt of court. On appeal, Lord Denning said: "There was no public interest in having the highly confidential documents in the present case made public. It was in the public interest that they should remain confidential. The use made of them by the journalist in the present case was highly detrimental to the good ordering of our society. They [were] used to launch a wholly unjustified attack on ministers of state and high civil servants who were only doing their best to deal with a wicked criminal."

That statement, one must remember, was made about the "disclosure" of a document that had already been read out in open court. It was made about someone who may have been a wicked criminal but was, at the time, in the custody of government officials, so that any cruelty to which he was subjected was a matter of public concern. But Harman's conviction was affirmed.

The outrage of the Harman case could not happen in Britain today. The law has caught up with the demands of a free society. Parliament passed a law making the provisions of the European Convention on Human Rights apply in British courts. One of those provisions calls for freedom of the press.

A case like Harriet Harman's could not have happened in the United States, not unless some distracted judge ignored the law—the law of the First Amendment. The use of the contempt power of judges to silence comment on legal matters was rejected by the Supreme Court in 1941 in the historic case of *Bridges v. California.*

Harry Bridges was the left-wing leader of the West Coast longshoremen's union. When a California state judge decided a case that affected his union in a way he did not like, Bridges sent a telegram to the U.S. secretary of labor criticizing the decision. The judge held him in contempt of court for that criticism. The Supreme Court considered the contempt order along with another from California, against the *Los Angeles Times.* Its offense was the publication of editorials about a criminal case in which two members of the Teamsters Union had been convicted of assault. The editorials said the trial judge would make "a serious mistake" if he sentenced them to probation; the community needed "the example of their assignment to the jute mill." (There was a fine irony in the coupling of the *Times* and Bridges on the same side in the Supreme Court. The *Times* was a strongly conservative, anti-union paper then, and its particular bête noir was Harry Bridges.)

In the Supreme Court, a drama was played out behind the scenes that only came into public view more than forty years later, in an exploration of Justice Black's papers after his

death. The case was first argued in October 1940. In conference, the justices voted 6 to 3 to affirm the two contempt convictions. Chief Justice Hughes assigned the majority opinion
to Justice Frankfurter. Frankfurter greatly admired English
law, and that came through in the draft opinion he circulated
to his colleagues. The power of judges to punish outside comment on matters pending in their courts, he said, is "part and
parcel of the Anglo-American system of administering justice.
. . . It is believed that all the judicatures of the English-speaking world . . . have from time to time recognized and exercised the power. . . . "

Justice Black circulated a dissent that said:

[T]he basic fallacy of the Court's opinion is the assumption
that the vitalizing liberties of the First Amendment can be
abridged . . . by reference to English judicial practice. . . . In
my judgment, to measure the scope of the liberties guaranteed by the First Amendment by the limitations that exist or
have existed throughout the English-speaking world is to
obtain a result directly opposite to that which the framers of
the Amendment intended. . . . Perhaps no single purpose
emerges more clearly from the history of our Constitution
and Bill of Rights than that of giving far more security to the
people of the United States with respect to freedom of religion, conscience, expression, assembly, petition and press
than the people of Great Britain had ever enjoyed. . . . The
First Amendment is proof conclusive that the framers of our
government were well aware of the suppression of conscience and expression that had been indulged in abroad,

both in England and elsewhere, and intended by the First Amendment to see that they did not happen here.

In the spring of 1941 one justice in the *Bridges* majority retired, and another changed his mind. That made the vote 4 to 4, and the Court ordered the case reargued the following fall. Before then Hughes retired, so it was 4 to 3 for reversal of the contempt convictions. Two new justices split, Robert H. Jackson for reversal and James F. Byrnes to uphold the convictions. Justice Black had a 5-to-4 majority and now wrote the opinion of the Court.

The *Bridges* decision was announced by the Supreme Court on December 8, 1941. The justices went on the bench after walking over to the Capitol in the morning to hear President Roosevelt denounce the Japanese attack on Pearl Harbor. ("Yesterday, December seventh, 1941, a date which will live in infamy. . . . ") In the circumstances, the decision did not get much attention. But it was in fact a turning point in constitutional history. It was the opening round in years of conflict between Justices Black and Frankfurter over whether the First Amendment guarantee of freedom of speech should be read broadly, as Black urged, or in a more limited way. The majority opinion in the *Bridges* case was a declaration of independence from the English legal tradition. That revolution was carried on twenty-three years later in *New York Times v. Sullivan*, breaking decisively with the English common-law rules that heavily favored libel plaintiffs.

The American press has been given extraordinary freedom by the Supreme Court's interpretations of the First Amendment.

In return, it owes society courage. It must resist the lure of obeisance to power. Its reporters and editors must remain freebooters—vagabonds and outlaws, as Bernard Levin put it. Only then can they perform the press's patriotic function of holding government to account.

10

Thoughts That
We Hate

It was in the case of a pacifist that Justice Holmes spoke of "freedom for the thought that we hate." But suppose it were not a pacifist but a Nazi. Would that change her right to freedom of expression? Should it?

Hate speech, it is called: virulent attacks on Jews, blacks, Muslims, homosexuals, or members of any other group. It is pure hatred, not based on any wrong done by an individual. A German may have been a practicing Roman Catholic; but if the Nazis found that he had a Jewish grandfather, off he went to a death camp.

The United States differs from almost all other Western societies in its legal treatment of hate speech. In Germany it is a crime, a serious one, to display the swastika or any other Nazi symbol. In eleven European countries it is a crime to say that the Holocaust did not happen, that Germans in the Nazi years did not slaughter Jews. So it is in Canada, and the Canadian Supreme

Court has decided that Holocaust deniers can be prosecuted and punished despite that country's constitutional guarantee of free expression. In the United States, the First Amendment protects the right to deny the fact of the Holocaust.

At one point the Supreme Court took a different view of bans on hateful speech. In 1952, in the case of *Beauharnais v. Illinois*, it sustained an Illinois law that made it a crime to distribute any publication that "portrays depravity, criminality, unchastity or lack of virtue of a class of citizens, of any race, color, creed or religion," exposing them to contempt or being "productive of breach of the peace or riots." Joseph Beauharnais had distributed a leaflet urging Chicago authorities to stop the "invasion of white . . . neighborhoods and persons by the Negro."

Justice Frankfurter, writing the opinion for a 5–4 majority, saw the Illinois law as a group form of criminal libel—which had existed in the American states from the beginning. "Illinois did not have to look beyond her own borders or await the tragic experience of the last three decades," Frankfurter said, "to conclude that wilful purveyors of falsehood concerning racial and religious groups promote strife. . . . " He instanced the murder in 1837 of Elijah Parish Lovejoy, a newspaper editor in Alton, in southern Illinois, because he favored the abolition of slavery, and recent race riots in the Chicago area. "Libellous utterances," he said, were not "within the area of constitutionally protected speech." Justice Black, dissenting, said that the Illinois law was entirely different from statutes against libel of individuals, and much more subject to abuse. Any minority group that welcomed the decision, he said, should remember Pyrrhus's statement: "Another such victory and I am undone."

The logical premise of Justice Frankfurter's *Beauharnais* opinion was undone by the 1964 decision in *New York Times v. Sullivan*, which ended the exclusion of libel from the protection of the First Amendment. Under *Sullivan* and cases stemming from it, public officials and public figures cannot recover damages for libel unless they can prove that a false statement of fact was published knowingly or recklessly. The generalized smear of hate speech—a Beauharnais pamphlet, for example—does not lend itself to the factual analysis contemplated by these later decisions, however vicious the smear may have been. That was so, the Court indicated, even when the viciousness was directed at an individual, as in *Hustler* magazine's attack on Jerry Falwell.

Moreover, the Court in 1969 put extremely tight restrictions on criminal punishment for speech attacking racial or religious groups. That was the case of *Brandenburg v. Ohio*, discussed in Chapter 7. The speaker there, a Ku Klux Klan leader, said, "Personally, I believe the nigger should be returned to Africa, the Jew returned to Israel." The Supreme Court unanimously reversed his conviction because there was no proof that the speaker was inciting "imminent lawless action" or that such action was likely to occur.

The issue of free speech for Nazis is symbolized in American law by the word "Skokie." Skokie is a village near Chicago that in 1977 had a large Jewish population, including a substantial number who were survivors of Nazi concentration camps. An American Nazi party announced that it would hold a demonstration in Skokie, with the demonstrators wearing a swastika, the Hitler symbol. The village authorities passed ordinances that among other things prohibited the dissemination of anything, including signs and clothing, that "incites hatred against persons by reason of their race, national origin, or religion." The authorities also sought an injunction to the same effect from the Illinois courts. Cases went through state and federal courts. The ultimate judgment was by the United States Court of Appeals for the Seventh Circuit, which held that the village ordinances designed to stop the demonstration were unconstitutional. The Nazi group then canceled its plan.

The Skokie episode created wide controversy among civil libertarians. Many members of the American Civil Liberties Union resigned because the ACLU had supported the Nazis' right to march. But the ACLU leadership did not budge, and in the end its stand probably improved its public standing and enlarged its membership.

Roger Errera, a French legal scholar and jurist, said that Europeans would not accept American tolerance for hateful speech, as in the Skokie case. The American view, he suggested, must be based on "an inveterate social and historical optimism"—which Europeans could not be expected to share after their tragic experience at the hands of the Nazis and Communists. Hitler had made his murderous intentions plain enough in *Mein Kampf.* Wouldn't it have been better to imprison him for such expression before he could organize his words into horrendous reality?

That is the dominant view in Europe, but it is not the only one. *The Economist,* the British weekly with an orientation toward the United States, made strong arguments in 2006 against laws criminalizing Holocaust denial and other forms of racist speech. Such laws, it warned, could be interpreted to punish or restrain speech that "merely causes offense." It instanced the example of Oriana Fallaci, the great Italian journalist, who when she died in 2006 was awaiting trial for offending Islam in a critical essay about the religion. "The big danger," *The Economist* wrote, "is that, in the name of stopping bigots, one may end up by stopping all criticism."

A notorious English Holocaust-denier, David Irving, served thirteen months in an Austrian prison in 2006–2007 for speeches he made in that country. Irving had sued an American author, Deborah Lipstadt, for libel for calling him a denier; an English judge, in a devastating judgment, found that the characterization was true. But Lipstadt said she regretted his imprisonment in Austria, which made him "a martyr to free speech."

The conflict over how to deal with hate speech grew more intense with the rise of Islamic extremism and terrorist acts at the beginning of the twenty-first century. Britain, one of several European countries with a substantial Muslim population, faced the issue particularly acutely. A number of imams allegedly urged violent jihad in sermons in their mosques. One was prosecuted and convicted for soliciting murder and racial hatred. A leader of a British Islamist group, Atilla Ahmet, said: "You are attacking our people in Muslim countries, in Iraq, in Afghanistan. So it's legitimate to attack British soldiers and policemen, government officials and even the White House." In July 2005 four Muslim suicide bombers killed fifty-two people in London subways and on a bus. A militant spokesman, Abu Izzadeen, called the bombings "praiseworthy." In 2007 he was arrested for a later speech and charged with encouraging terrorism.

The great statement of reasons for allowing even the most noxious speech was made by Brandeis in his opinion in *Whitney v. California:* "Discussion affords ordinarily adequate protection against the dissemination of noxious doctrine," he wrote. And, "The fitting remedy for evil counsels is good ones." But even the Supreme Court's highly tolerant decision in *Brandenburg v. Ohio* in 1969 would allow legal action against speech that is intended to incite imminent lawlessness and is likely to do so. Doesn't a call for the murder of police and other officials pass that test, given the fact of actual murders in the Islamist cause? Given the context—an actual terrorist bombing in Britain—the *Brandenburg* requirement of imminence seems to me inappropriate.

One of the arguments for allowing hateful speech is that it makes the rest of us aware of terrible beliefs and strengthens our resolve to combat them. This argument was rudely countered by Jeremy Waldron, an Englishman who emigrated to teach law in the United States. He wrote:

> The costs of hate speech . . . are not spread evenly across the community that is supposed to tolerate them. The [racists] of the world may not harm the people who call for their toleration, but then few of them are depicted as animals in posters plastered around Leamington Spa [an English town]. We should speak to those who are depicted in this way, or those whose suffering or whose parents' suffering is mocked

by the [Skokie neo-Nazis] before we conclude that tolerating this sort of speech builds character.

Something like Jeremy Waldron's view animated a movement, in the 1980s and 1990s, to ban hateful speech on university campuses. Spurred by members of minority groups, the movement aimed at racist speech. Proponents of banning hate speech against minorities said students who were victimized by such speech were traumatized by it. To deal with the problem, some professors and students called for the adoption of speech codes, with penalties for violations.

A significant number of universities adopted speech codes. In practice, they dealt with hurtful comments on a wide range of matters beyond the original proposal, race. One of the best-known codes, adopted by Stanford University, prohibited "harassment by personal vilification" when it was "intended to stigmatize an individual or a small number of individuals on the basis of their sex, race, color, handicap, religion, sexual orientation, or national and ethnic origin." A code proposed by the University of Massachusetts at Amherst in 1995 added to those subjects "age, marital status, veteran status." The graduate students' union there wanted to add "citizenship, culture, H.I.V. status, language, parental status, political belief and pregnancy."

The lengthening list of characteristics to be protected from harassing speech brought ridicule on the speech-code campaign. In 1989 a federal court held the University of Michigan code unconstitutional. Stanford's failed a legal test a few years later. And the campaign ebbed.

No one can doubt that black students and others had historically been subjected to viciousness at some universities, not limited to speech. But once the attempt to deal with the problem by speech codes got going, it became too easy a target for critics of political correctness. Even a sense of humor seemed endangered. A Harvard Law School professor drew protests when he quoted an opinion by Justice Robert H. Jackson. The trouble was that Jackson had used a quote from a poem by Byron: the famous lines about Julia, "who, swearing she would ne'er consent, consented."

The attempt to censor what is said at universities has not been limited to such foolishness. In 2003 the House of Representatives passed a bill called the International Studies in Higher Education Act. It would have required the secretary of education, in allocating federal funds to universities, to consider whether foreign language or area studies courses reflected diverse perspectives. It would have created an advisory board to "study, monitor, appraise and evaluate" university programs supported by federal funds. A principal supporter of the bill, Representative Howard Berman of California, said he was concerned about "anti-American bias" in Middle East studies programs. There was evidence, he said, that many Middle East studies grantees had a point of view that "questions the validity of advancing American ideals of democracy and the rule of law" in the Middle East and elsewhere.

Most American colleges and universities get federal aid of one kind or another. Under such legislation, their faculties and administrators would have had to worry about whether their classes conformed to the ideas, and very likely the ideology, of a federal board. Yet the very premise of Representative Berman's argument for it, that "advancing American ideals of democracy" in the Middle East was a wise idea, was controversial, to put it mildly. That premise played a large part in creating the disaster of the Iraq War. Universities above all should be places where ideas are challenged.

The largest controversy about offensive speech in modern America concerned not a verbal utterance but symbolic expression: burning the flag. During the Republican National Convention in 1984 a group of demonstrators marched through the streets protesting the policies of the Reagan administration. One of them, Gregory Lee Johnson, set an American flag on fire in front of the Dallas City Hall. He was convicted of violating a Texas law that prohibited desecration of a "venerated object." The Supreme Court, by a vote of 5 to 4, reversed his conviction, finding the flag-burning expressive conduct that was protected by the First Amendment. "If there is a bedrock principle underlying the First Amendment," Justice Brennan wrote in the opinion of the Court, "it is that the government may not prohibit the expression of an idea simply because society finds the idea itself offensive or disagreeable."

Many Americans indeed found the burning of the flag offensive. Congress came close to approving a constitutional amendment to allow the criminalizing of flag-burning. It did pass a criminal statute, the Flag Protection Act of 1989, to punish anyone who, except to dispose of a worn or soiled flag, "mutilates, defaces, physically defiles, burns, maintains on the floor or ground, or tramples upon any flag of the United States." In *United States v. Eichman* in 1990 the Supreme

Court, by the identical 5–4 vote, held that statute unconstitutional. Justice Brennan, writing again for the majority, said the very list of prohibitions showed that the concern behind the act was "disrespectful treatment" of the flag. Thus the act "suppresses expression out of concern for its likely communicative impact." Justice Brennan concluded: "Punishing desecration of the flag dilutes the very freedom that makes this emblem so revered, and worth revering."

In the catalog of hateful or offensive expression, burning a flag is surely less dangerous than most other examples: anti-Semitic ravings in a Munich beer hall, say, or preaching to young Muslims in England that they should become suicide-bombers. (One worshipper who heard such sermons, Richard Reid, tried unsuccessfully to blow up an airliner with a bomb in his shoe.)

In 1994 broadcasts on a radio station in Rwanda urged Hutus, who were a majority of the population, to kill Tutsis, the minority, and moderate-minded Hutus. A massacre followed, and more than 500,000 people were killed. Years later a Tutsi-led government forbade political parties to appeal to group identity, and public statements promoting "divisionism" were outlawed. Should we in America who have avoided such tragedies tell Rwandans that it is wrong for them thus to limit freedom of speech?

In an age when words have inspired acts of mass murder and terrorism, it is not as easy for me as it once was to believe that the only remedy for evil counsels, in Brandeis's phrase, should be good ones. The law of the American Constitution allows suppression only when violence or violation of law are intended by speakers and are likely to take place imminently. But perhaps judges, and the rest of us, will be more on guard now for the rare act of expression—not the burning of a flag or the racist slang of an undergraduate—that is genuinely dangerous. I think we should be able to punish speech that urges terrorist violence to an audience some of whose members are ready to act on the urging. That is imminence enough.

11

Balancing Interests

Since the middle of the twentieth century, the idea of the First Amendment has acquired a powerful hold on the American imagination. Even conservatives, who had been found on the repressive side of speech controversies, now join in exaltation of freedom of expression. People invoke "the First Amendment" as if those words would settle whatever issue was being debated. But in truth the freedoms of speech and of the press have never been absolutes. The courts and society have repeatedly struggled to accommodate other interests along with those.

A long-running example is the effort to square freedom of the press with protection of the right to fair trial. How can a defendant get an unbiased jury if newspapers and broadcasters have convicted him in graphic terms before the trial begins? The Supreme Court dealt with the issue over a period of nearly forty years. Once again, the starting point was English practice.

In 1949 a series of murder victims were found in London with bite marks in their necks. Inevitably, the popular papers called the unknown murderer "the vampire killer." On March

4, 1949, the *Daily Mirror*, then the largest-selling tabloid, carried the headline: "Vampire—A Man Held." The lead, a tabloid classic of its day, said: "The Vampire Killer will never strike again. He is safely behind bars, powerless to lure victims to a hideous death. This is the assurance which the *Daily Mirror* can give today. It is the considered conclusion of the finest detective brains in the country." The story did not give the name of the person "safely behind bars." But on an inside page, a short piece said a man called John George Haigh was helping the police with their inquiries— tabloidese for being questioned by the police—in an unidentified criminal investigation.

The editor of the *Mirror* was Silvester Bolam, known to his colleagues as Bishop Bolam because he habitually wore a black suit and white shirt. Bolam was summoned to court, where a judge sentenced him to three months in prison for contempt by endangering a suspect's fair trial. Bolam was taken from the courtroom to serve his sentence, and he never worked in journalism again.

That was the British system for discouraging pretrial comment in criminal cases: short and sharp. And it still is, though erring editors are now more likely to be fined than imprisoned. That is what happened, for example, when the *Sunday People* said the way to protect the Queen from marauders in Buckingham Palace was "Give Her a Cuddle, Philip" (see Chapter 9).

The reality in America is different. In 1977 a serial murderer in New York signed notes "Son of Sam." When a suspect, David Berkowitz, was arrested, the *New York Post*'s headline, in red, was: "Caught!" The story named him and said he told the police that he was on the way to kill more victims when he was arrested. Nothing happened to the editor of the *Post.*

American law broke with the stern British view of public comment on pending cases in the 1941 decision in *Bridges v. California,* also described in Chapter 9. The Supreme Court held that such comment could not be punished as contempt unless there was a "clear and present danger" of perverting the course of justice—and no case after that found such a danger. The use of contempt as a device to discourage reporting that might endanger the fairness of a future trial was effectively barred.

But the problem of prejudicial press coverage of sensational cases remained. What else could be done about it? In 1961 the Supreme Court for the first time tried another course. It held that the Constitution required reversal of a murder conviction when pretrial publicity had made a fair trial unlikely. The case was *Irvin v. Dowd,* and the facts were extreme. The defendant was called "the mad dog killer" by the press. When jurors were questioned before the trial, eight of twelve said they thought he was guilty from what they had read—but believed they could still decide on the evidence in court.

Justice Frankfurter, who had dissented in the *Bridges* case, still wanted to take direct action against the press—as he made bitterly clear in a separate opinion: "This Court has not yet decided that the fair administration of justice must be subordinated to another safeguard of our constitutional system—freedom of the press, properly conceived. The Court has not yet decided that, while convictions must be reversed and miscarriages of justice result because the minds of jurors or potential jurors were poisoned, the poisoner is constitutionally protected in plying his trade." That was wishful thinking on Justice Frankfurter's part. The Court had in fact decided that what he called the poisoner, the press, was constitutionally protected—at least against British-style contempt punishment.

Reversal of a conviction was an awkward way to deal with the effects of sensational stories on a jury. By the time an appellate court made such a decision, witnesses might have died or disappeared. The Supreme Court suggested alternatives in the case of Dr. Samuel Sheppard, which became famous in a romanticized movie version, *The Fugitive*. Doctor Sam, as the press called him, was charged with the murder of his wife at their home in a Cleveland, Ohio, suburb in 1954. The press had played a vigorous part in demanding his arrest and prosecution. A front-page editorial was entitled, "Quit Stalling— Bring Him In." In a radio broadcast, a commentator compared Sheppard to Alger Hiss, who was accused of being a Soviet spy in a notorious case of the time. At the trial, reporters filled the courtroom. Jurors and witnesses were photographed and televised when they entered or left the court.

When *Sheppard v. Maxwell* (1966) reached the Supreme Court, Justice Tom C. Clark wrote that "bedlam reigned at the courthouse during the trial." The Court concluded that Sheppard had been denied "the judicial serenity and calm" to which he was entitled as a defendant. It set aside his conviction. Justice Clark, writing for the Court, went on to suggest ways of preventing such travesties. Trial judges could bar statements to the press by the police, prosecutors, and defense counsel. They could and should control the scene in the courtroom. If there was prejudicial publicity, they could delay the trial or move it to another location—a change of venue. They could sequester the jury, insulating it from public comment.

There is a striking curiosity in the Sheppard case. Sheppard was convicted in 1954, and the Ohio courts finally upheld the conviction in 1956. That same year the Supreme Court denied a petition for review. But ten years later the Court agreed to hear an appeal, on a petition for habeas corpus by Sheppard's lawyers, and set aside his conviction. Why did the Court change its mind and act a decade later?

The habeas corpus petition focused on the prejudicial effect of the press behavior before and during the trial. My guess is that the justices found that issue compelling in 1966 because of a powerful intervening event: the assassination of President Kennedy and then the murder, in Dallas police headquarters, of the alleged assassin, Lee Harvey Oswald. Chief Justice Warren was the chairman of the commission that investigated the assassination and its aftermath. The commission wrote stingingly about the behavior of the press in Dallas, among other things its overwhelming presence in police headquarters—which may have helped Jack Ruby come in and shoot Oswald.

The next idea tried out on the fair trial–free press issue was to bar the press, by injunction, from publishing anything before trial that was strongly "implicative of guilt" on the part of an accused. The case arose from the gruesome murder of six family members in the small town of Sutherland, Nebraska, in 1975 in connection with a sexual assault. A suspect named Erwin Charles Simants was arrested, and there was quite naturally intense press interest in the case, local and national. The prosecutor and Simants's lawyer joined in asking the Nebraska courts to limit press coverage lest it become impossible to pick an unprejudiced jury. The Nebraska Supreme Court prohibited reporting of any confession by Simants (who had in fact made one) or other matters "strongly implicative" of him.

The Supreme Court of the United States reviewed that order in 1976. There was considerable expectation that it would approve some restraints on reporting. Other courts had begun issuing such injunctions in aggravated criminal cases. (The press called them "gag orders," a characterization that made them seem illegitimate.) But the Supreme Court did not do so. The Court's opinion, by Chief Justice Burger, said that "prior restraints on speech and publication are the most serious and least tolerable infringement on First Amendment Rights." It ruled out injunctions against press coverage of criminal proceedings before trial unless there was a "clear and present danger" of preventing a fair trial. That always elusive phrase did not really hide the fact that the decision, *Nebraska Press Association v. Stuart*, was a great victory for the press. If a bar on publishing a confession was wrong in so aggravated a situation—a gruesome multiple murder in a small rural town—it was hard to see when one would be permissible. And in fact, none was sustained on appeal after that.

Three years later one more proposal to prevent the prejudicing of juries was tried out. At a pretrial hearing in a murder case in upstate New York, defense counsel moved to close the courtroom to the public, including the press. The prosecutor did not object; and the judge, Daniel A. DePasquale, granted the motion. The Gannett newspaper chain did object, and the case went to the Supreme Court in 1979 as *Gannett Co. v. DePasquale.*

By a vote of 5 to 4, the Court upheld the order closing the courtroom. The majority opinion focused not on the First but on the Sixth Amendment, which says among other things, "In all criminal prosecutions, the accused shall enjoy the right to a speedy and public trial." Justice Stewart said the public-trial right could be invoked only by the defendant, who had waived it in this case, not by outsiders like the press. "Members of the public," he wrote, "have no constitutional right under the Sixth and Fourteenth Amendments to attend criminal trials." For the dissenters, Justice Harry Blackmun disagreed about the Sixth Amendment in an analysis that sounded more like a discussion of the First. The guarantee of public trial, he said, ensures that everyone in the criminal justice system is "subjected to public scrutiny." He said pretrial hearings, like the one in this case, often consider charges of misconduct by the police—and were the only chance for the public to learn about possible official misconduct. He noted that most criminal cases are ended by a plea before trial; in this county, Seneca, not one prosecution went on to a trial in 1976.

The *Gannett* decision was greeted with a chorus of outrage by the press. The chairman of the American Newspaper Publishers Association said it showed that the Supreme Court was "determined to unmake the Constitution." Several members of the Court indicated, unusually, that they were troubled by the criticism.

One year to the day after its *Gannett* decision, the Court reversed its field. In *Richmond Newspapers v. Virginia* it considered the same question, whether courtrooms can be closed to protect the sanctity of juries, under the First Amendment. By a vote of 8 to 1, the Court said the speech and press clauses of the amendment assured the public's right to attend trials. (At the argument, Professor Laurence Tribe of the Harvard Law School, representing the newspapers, had disclaimed any special right of access for the press.) There was no majority opinion. But Justice John Paul Stevens put his finger on the larger significance of the case in a concurring opinion: "Until today the Court has accorded virtually absolute protection to the dissemination of information or ideas, but never before has it squarely held that the acquisition of newsworthy matter is entitled to any constitutional protection whatsoever."

The potential reach of the new constitutional theory that Justice Stevens described was revolutionary. With a right of access under the First Amendment, the press could sue to see secret government documents and attend closed meetings. So it might have seemed. The reality was not like that at all. The Supreme Court confined the new right to situations where there was a tradition of openness—like court proceedings. Attempts to get into other matters failed.

There the effort to find some constitutional way of insulating juries from outside comment stood: in frustration. The Supreme Court had been unable to resolve the tension between the interests of fair trial and freedom of the press—and let the latter prevail.

That is just an example of the many subjects in which freedom of expression has been in tension with other important interests. Another is the effort to limit the corrupting effect of financing political campaigns. The issue is complex enough to justify an entire book. Here it can have only the briefest of summaries.

No other democratic society allows political campaigns remotely as expensive as those in the United States. By the twenty-first century, presidential candidates of the major parties were spending in excess of $100 million just for the primaries and other early stages. In 1971 and 1974, Congress passed legislation intended to control the race for funding— and the influence-peddling that accompanied it. The legislation put limits on individual contributions to candidates, and on expenditures by candidates and by others on their behalf.

In 1976, in the case of *Buckley v. Valeo*, the Supreme Court considered claims that the ceilings violated the First Amendment's guarantees of freedom of expression. The Court upheld limits on contributions, but it found the expenditure ceilings unconstitutional. Political spending, it said, was a form of speech at the heart of the First Amendment. The unsigned opinion said the amendment "denies government the power to determine that spending to promote one's political views is wasteful, excessive, or unwise." The result was to give a great advantage to candidates with personal wealth and to those who were good at attracting contributions. Criticism of the decision was summed up wittily by Professor Paul A. Freund of the Harvard Law School, the leading constitutional scholar of his day: "They say that money talks. I thought that was the problem, not the solution."

Before long, politicians and their supporters had bored loopholes in the contribution limits that the Supreme Court had upheld. In 2002 Congress made a new attempt to stem the flood of money. It banned what had been unlimited contributions to the political parties, and it outlawed some television advertising paid for by corporations and labor unions during campaigns. Critics from right to left—from the National Rifle Association to the American Civil Liberties Union—objected that the law violated the First Amendment. But the Supreme Court rejected the critics' claims. There were multiple opinions and differing judicial lineups, by votes of 5 to 4—an indication of how sharp the tension was between the conflicting interests of campaign reform and freedom of expression. Despite the legal victory for reform, the reality was that campaign spending kept going up. Its heaviest cost, even worse than the opportunities for corruption, was the burden the money race put on politicians. In 2007 the Supreme Court, with two new members, turned away from reform. It held that restrictions on political spending by independent entities in the period just before the elections violated the First Amendment. Members of the Senate and House had to spend endless time raising money for their next campaigns.

The role of the First Amendment in election campaigns arose in a different context: elections of judges. Most states elect their judges, unlike the appointive system followed in other Western countries and in the federal government. (The federal practice was based on the Massachusetts constitution of 1780, which was drafted by John Adams and is still in force.)

Judicial elections used to be tame affairs, attracting little attention. In states where judges had fixed terms or had to face a periodic vote on whether they should continue, incumbents routinely won. But toward the end of the twentieth century, conservative political forces realized that judicial decisions had an impact on issues that mattered to them: social issues such as abortion as well as economic ones like punitive damages. So the conservatives opposed some sitting judges, spent increasing amounts of money to beat them, and succeeded in doing so in many cases.

To limit the politicization of judicial elections, many states adopted rules that barred judicial candidates from stating their views on controversial issues: "I am against abortion" and the like. Minnesota had what it called the "announce clause," forbidding candidates for judgeships to announce their views on legal or political issues. The Republican Party of Minnesota challenged the rule as a violation of the First Amendment, and won in the Supreme Court in 2002. By a vote of 5 to 4, the Court held that politicization of the courts, if it increased, was a price that had to be paid for our system of free speech. Similar rules in many other states were overthrown by the decision. And the cost of judicial elections, which used to be negligible, rose sharply—to over $1 million in campaigns for state supreme court justices.

The Minnesota decision seems to me an egregious misapplication of the First Amendment, treating it woodenly and ignoring the reality involved. The test of judicial decisions is not, as Justice Holmes said of political speech, "the power of the thought to get itself accepted in the competition of the market." Some of the greatest judicial opinions have run against popular opinion—as did those of Holmes and Brandeis when they dissented from the punishment of radical speech. If judges announce their views in election campaigns, in effect telling the voters that they will decide this way or that, they appear to be just another species of politician. The commitment of judges should be to the law, to interpreting it as faithfully as they can, and not to current popular opinion.

When the Supreme Court reaches a debated result by a narrow margin, as in the Minnesota case, there is always a hope among those disappointed by the result that a later Court may overrule the decision. Indeed, it can be more than hope. Opponents of *Roe v. Wade*, the 1973 case upholding a woman's right to choose abortion on constitutional grounds, campaigned fiercely for that decision to be overruled. The Court has said that its constitutional decisions are always open to reconsideration in light of experience and new understandings.

Chief Justice Hughes spoke of dissents as appeals "to the brooding spirit of the law." He described as "self-inflicted wounds" three Supreme Court decisions that had profoundly damaging consequences for the country and the Court itself—decisions that in different ways were overturned.

The first of the three was the Dred Scott case, in which Chief Justice Roger B. Taney wrote in 1857 that black people could not be citizens of the United States. It was overruled by the Civil War and the Fourteenth Amendment, which provides that all persons born in the United States are citizens. The second was one of the legal tender cases of 1869, in which a divided Court held that paper money was unconstitutional; it was overruled by the Court itself two years later. The third came in 1895, when a federal income tax (of 2 percent) was held unconstitutional. That decision was overturned by the Sixteenth Amendment in 1913.

The Court has reversed itself more often lately than in earlier years. A well-known example was the 2003 decision in *Lawrence v. Texas*, overruling a 1986 decision and holding that the states could not criminalize homosexual sodomy. But it is still a notable occasion when the Supreme Court changes its mind. And since the ascendancy of the First Amendment, it has not changed its mind about the central importance of freedom of speech or of the press. The abortion decision, *Roe v. Wade*, has been whittled away; but *New York Times v. Sullivan* and other landmarks of free expression stand unchanged.

12

Freedom of Thought

The freedom of speech and press promised by the First
Amendment is not only external but internal: not only "freedom of expression" but "freedom of thought." The latter phrase
was used as shorthand for America's promise even before the
Constitution. A few weeks after the Declaration of Independence was issued in 1776, Samuel Adams, John's cousin, the fiery
orator whose speeches helped to set off the Revolution, told an
audience in Philadelphia: "Driven from every corner of the
earth, freedom of thought and the right of private judgment in
matters of conscience direct their course to this happy country
for their last asylum."

Why do we want freedom of thought, of speech and press?
The reasons have been canvassed by philosophers and judges
and professors. Professor Zechariah Chafee Jr., whose writing
on freedom of speech so influenced Justice Holmes, divided the
subject into two large categories. "The First Amendment," he
wrote, "protects two kinds of interests in free speech. There is
an individual interest, the need of many men to express their

opinions on matters vital to them if life is to be worth living, and a social interest in the attainment of truth. . . . "

Through a long history, individuals have struggled against repressive forces to express themselves. Their need to speak, as Chafee put it, may have been scientific in origin, or literary, or political. Galileo wanted to publish what he had proved by observation: that the earth moved around the sun. He was finally silenced by the repressive arm of the Catholic hierarchy at the time, the Inquisition. (The story is movingly told in Bertolt Brecht's play *Galileo*.) Boris Pasternak, after years of silence during Stalin's terror in the Soviet Union, wrote *Doctor Zhivago*, managed to have it published abroad, and won the Nobel Prize. But even after Stalin's death, official pressure forced him to renounce his acceptance of the prize. Anita Whitney rebelled against her socially prominent family and courted danger by helping to found the Communist Labor Party of California. Her criminal conviction evoked Justice Brandeis's great statement on free speech.

Perhaps there is something especially American about the need for self-expression if life is to be worth living, as Chafee put it. Albert Einstein used the same phrase in describing what he found when he came to the United States. "From what I have seen of Americans," he wrote in 1944, "I think that life would not be worth living without this freedom of self-expression."

The social interest in freedom of thought has been put in many different ways, most prominently in what Chafee called the interest in the attainment of truth. John Stuart Mill, in his

"On Liberty" in 1859, laid the philosophical groundwork. He argued that a suppressed opinion may contain a whole or partial truth that society needs. Even a false belief is valuable, he argued, because the process of debate about it may test and confirm the truth of the opposing view.

Justice Holmes gave powerful expression to Mill's argument in his *Abrams* dissent in 1919: Men may come to believe, he wrote, "that the ultimate good desired is better reached by free trade in ideas—that the best test of truth is the power of the thought to get itself accepted in the competition of the market." (The phrase "marketplace of ideas" is often used as if it were Holmes's, but he did not exactly say that. Professor Vincent Blasi traced the phrase and found its first use in a letter to the editor of the *New York Times* from David M. Newbold in 1936.)

Unlike many advocates of free speech as a search engine for truth, Holmes was really prepared to risk severe consequences. Professor Blasi put it:

Holmes, the old soldier and proud Darwinist, thought that one of the valuable functions of dissenting speech, including speech that advocates violent revolution, is its capacity to generate some of the grievances, aspirations and mobilizations that force political adaptation and transformation. . . . Probably the most energizing contribution that the freedom of speech can make is simply to leave people free to follow their political thoughts wherever they might lead—free, that is, to think the unthinkable regarding political loyalty, consent, obedience and violence.

James Madison saw freedom of speech, and especially of the press, as essential in a republic—a political system in which "the people, not the government, possess the absolute sovereignty." Madison's latter-day apostle of political freedom, the philosopher Alexander Meiklejohn, said in 1948: "When men govern themselves, it is they—and no one else—who must pass judgment upon unwisdom and unfairness and danger." Thus, for Meiklejohn, no restraint on political speech could be squared with the First Amendment.

A particular aspect of the case for freedom in political speech is what Blasi called "the checking value"—the role of the press and commentators in pointing to, and correcting, abuses of official power. The checking value has become crucial as the imperial pretensions of the executive branch of government have grown ever greater. When President George W. Bush took the United States to war in Iraq on false premises, and then secretly ordered the wiretapping of Americans in violation of law and claimed the right to torture detainees, Congress seemed unable or unwilling to perform the checking role that Madison and the other Framers of the Constitution had envisaged. It was the press that eventually penetrated the secrecy and exposed the abuses. And Bush has not been the only president with imperial ambitions and an exalted view of his power.

A final argument for broad freedom of expression is its effect on the character of individuals in a society. Citizens in a free society must have courage—the courage to hear not only unwelcome political speech but novel and shocking ideas in science and the arts. In his opinion in the *Whitney* case, Brandeis sounded the theme of civic courage:

Those who won our independence by revolution were not cowards. They did not fear political change. They did not exalt order at the cost of liberty. To courageous, self-reliant men, with confidence in the power of free and fearless reasoning applied though the processes of popular government, no danger flowing from speech can be deemed clear and present, unless the incidence of the evil apprehended is so imminent that it may befall before there is opportunity for full discussion. . . .

The courage required in a free society is not alone of those who believe in change, but of journalists and other shapers of opinion. And, not least, of judges. Many of the great advances in the quality—the decency—of American society were initiated by judges: on racial justice, on respect for the equal humanity of women and homosexuals, on freedom of speech itself. Every one of such steps exposed judges to bitter words and, sometimes, physical danger. "We are very quiet there," Holmes said of the Supreme Court, "but it is the quiet of a storm center."

Attacks on the courts grew in ferocity in the latter part of the twentieth century. Much of the antagonism came from those white southerners who wanted to defend their racist institutions from the civil rights progress set in motion by the 1954 Supreme Court decision in *Brown v. Board of Education* that racial segregation in public schools was unconstitutional. The attackers sought to delegitimize the Court and its members. Later, it was decisions upholding the free-speech rights of radicals that brought outcries.

Conservatives used the word "activist" to denounce what they did not like—"activist judges," "activist decisions." The word implied that judges had gone beyond their proper role in interpreting the Constitution, but it was used with so little consistency that it was meaningless except as a way to denounce a result that the critic disliked. The truth is that bold judicial decisions have made the country what it is, from John Marshall's expansive vision of the nation to *Brown v. Board of Education.* Only that kind of judicial boldness—of courage—will preserve a free society in an age of international threats and of governments ready to use them to advance their own power.

Of course a democracy should not wait for courts to save it. Some threats to American freedom never came to a definitive judicial decision. The Sedition Act of 1798 was effectively rejected by the voters in the election of 1800. The Palmer Raids of 1920 finally aroused public discontent. The Supreme Court rejected a challenge to the removal of Japanese Americans from their West Coast homes in World War II, but Congress eventually apologized for the outrage. Public exposure killed one of the most insidious repressive government programs, a harassment system run by the longtime director of the FBI, J. Edgar Hoover. Hoover acted to ruin the lives of those he considered dangerous leftists. The program was exposed when an unknown group raided an FBI office in Media, Pennsylvania, in 1971 and released the name of the program, Cointelpro, and some of its damning actions. Even in a time of fear about communism, Cointelpro was insupportable in the sunlight—"the best of disinfectants," in Brandeis's words.

Secrecy and repression breed fear. Openness can make us confident. Justice Black's sister-in-law, Virginia Durr, put it well when she said of Black: "He felt that when people couldn't discuss issues, then nobody could be free. That's one reason I always had a feeling of safety around him."

In 2006, during the war in Iraq, a Pakistani woman, twenty-five-year-old Nur Fatima, moved to the United States. She settled in Brooklyn, where she was interviewed by a *New York Times* reporter, Andrea Elliott. She told the reporter: "I got freedom in this country. Freedom of everything. Freedom of thought."

Samuel Adams's vision of America still lives.

ACKNOWLEDGMENTS

Vincent Blasi and I have taught a course together at Columbia University's Graduate School of Journalism for the last twenty years. He is a professor of law at Columbia and the University of Virginia; the course is on the constitutional law of the press. Vince has educated me. And he did me an extraordinary kindness by reading the manuscript of this book and making many important suggestions. I owe him much.

The idea for the book came from Wendy Strothman, my literary agent, who went on to give me valuable advice. William Frucht, executive editor of Basic Books, made the idea reality. His assistant, Courtney Miller, was helpful, as were Basic's project editors, Shana Murph and Sandra Beris. The copy editor, Katherine Streckfus, did a wonderful job of correcting and provoking me.

Linda Greenhouse, who covers the Supreme Court for the *New York Times,* helped me puzzle out the elusive meaning of the Court's decisions. Over many years, librarians and researchers at the *New York Times* informed me.

Christina Mathers kept me straight on this project as on much else. My wife, Margaret Marshall, who is a judge, cast a professional and lovingly critical eye on every word.

Thank you all.

TABLE OF CASES

A v. B	77
Abrams v. U.S.	28
Allen v. Men's World	70
American Booksellers v. Hudnut	138
Barenblatt v. U.S.	116
Bartnicki v. Vopper	75
Beauharnais v. Illinois	158
Bond v. Floyd	126
Brandenburg v. Ohio	124
Branzburg v. Hayes	83
Bridges v. California	153, 171
Brown v. Board of Education	48, 187
Buckley v. Valeo	177
Burstyn v. Wilson & Co.	135
Buthelezi v. Poorter	93
Callender case	14
Cantwell v. Connecticut	111
City of Renton v. Playtime Theatres	137
Cohen v. California	42, 131
Cohen v. Cowles Media	90
Collin v. Smith	159
Cox Broadcasting v. Cohn	74
Debs v. U. S.	27
DeJonge v. Oregon	109
Dennis v. U.S.	120
Doubleday v. New York	133

Dred Scott v. Sanford — 180
Farber, Matter of — 95
FCC v. Pacifica — 137
Frohwerk v. U.S. — 27
Garland v. Torre — 81
Gannett Co. v. DePasquale — 175
Gertz v. Robert Welch — 57
Gitlow v. New York — 34, 108
Grosjean v. American Press — 46
Hepburn v. Griswold — 181
Herndon v. Lowry — 110
Home Building & Loan Assoc. v. Blaisdell — 41
Home Office v. Harman — 152
Hustler v. Falwell — 138
In re Grand Jury Subpoena — 98
Irvin v. Dowd — 171
Jacobellis v. Ohio — 136
Knauff v. Shaughnessy — 130
Korematsu v. U.S. — 113
Lamont v. Postmaster General — 124
Lawrence v. Texas — 181
Lingens v. Austria — xiii
Marbury v. Madison — 9
Masses Publishing v. Patten — 30
McConnell v. Federal Election Commission — 178
Melvin v. Reid — 73
Memoirs v. Massachusetts — 136
Midler v. Ford Motor Co. — 70
Miller v. California — 136
Minersville School District v. Gobitis — 114
Missouri v. Holland — 41
Near v. Minnesota — 43, 96
Nebraska Press Assoc. v. Stuart — 174
New York Times v. Sullivan — 48, 96, 159
New York Times v. U.S. — 47, 85

Olmstead v. U.S. 69
Onassis v. Dior 70
Patterson v. Colorado 24
Pentagon Papers: See N.Y. Times v. U.S.
Pollock v. Farmers' Loan & Trust Co. 181
Republican Party of Minnesota v. White 179
Richmond Newspapers v. Virginia 97, 176
Roe v. Wade 181
Roth v. U.S. 133
Scales v. U.S. 123
Schenck v. U.S. 26
Sheppard v. Maxwell 172
Shulman v. Group W 70
Sidis v. F-R Pub. Corp 60
Sipple v. Chronicle 72
Stromberg v. California 39
Sweezy v. New Hampshire 117
Texas v. Johnson 40, 165
Time Inc. v. Hill 62
U.S. v. Eichman 165
U.S. v. One Book Called "Ulysses" 133
U.S. v. Schwimmer xiv, 37
U.S. v. Wen Ho Lee 92
West Virginia Bd. of Educ. v. Barnette 114
Whitney v. California 35, 162, 187
Wooley v. Maynard 115
Yates v. U.S. 123

NOTES

The notes use legal methods of citation. Thus *United States v. Schwimmer*, 279 U.S. 644, 654–55 (1929), means that the Supreme Court decided the case in 1929 and that the opinions can be found starting at page 644 of volume 279 of the United States Reports, the official volumes of the Court's decisions; the particular passage quoted or mentioned in the text is on pages 654–55.

Introduction

   x *Hughes:* Speech in Elmira, N.Y., 1907.

  xii *Barak:* Remarks at the Hebrew University Honorary Doctorate Award Ceremony, June 7, 1998.

 xiii *Lingens case: Lingens v. Austria,* 8 E.H.H.R. 407, 409, 418–19 (1986).

 xiv *Holmes: United States v. Schwimmer,* 279 U.S. 644, 654–55 (1929).

 xiv *Justice Ginsburg's speech:* University of Cape Town, Feb. 10, 2006.

  xv *Wilton, Connecticut, school principal:* See New York Times, Mar. 10, 2007, p. 10, col. 1.

Chapter 1

  1 *King Henry's proclamation:* See Frederick Seaton Siebert, *Freedom of the Press in England, 1476–1776: The Rise and*

Decline of Government Controls 48 (University of Illinois Press, 1952).

2 *Milton:* John Milton, "Areopagitica: A Speech for the Liberty of Unlicensed Printing to the Parliament of England," para. 8.

3 *Blackstone:* Sir William Blackstone, *Commentaries on the Laws of England*, Bk. 4, Chap. 2, pp. 151–52 (1765–1769).

5 *Levy books: Legacy of Suppression* (Belknap Press of Harvard University Press 1960); *Emergence of a Free Press* 271 (Oxford University Press 1985).

7 *Quock Walker case:* See Peter W. Agnes Jr., *The Quork Walker Cases and the Abolition of Slavery in Massachusetts: A Reflection of Popular Sentiment or an Expression of Constitutional Law?* Boston Bar J., March-April 1992 at 8, 10. (Walker's first name was spelled in various ways.)

8 *Madison's letter to Jefferson:* Oct. 17, 1788.

9 *Jefferson's reply:* Mar. 15, 1789.

Chapter 2

12 *Abigail Adams:* James Morton Smith, *Freedom's Fetters* 96 (Cornell University Press 1956).

13 *Matthew Lyon:* James Morton Smith, *Freedom's Fetters: The Alien and Sedition Laws and American Civil Liberties* (Cornell University Press 1956), starting at p. 226.

14 *Callender case:* Ibid., starting at p. 334.

16 *Rep. John Allen's remarks:* Ibid., pp. 113–14.

16 *Gallatin's remarks:* Ibid., pp. 122–23, and Leonard W. Levy, *Emergence of a Free Press* 302–3 (Oxford University Press 1985).

16 *Nichols:* Levy, *Emergence of a Free Press* 301–2, 310.

17 *The Virginia Resolutions and Madison's Report:* The relevant one of the Virginia Resolutions is at 4 *Elliot's Debates on the Federal Constitution* 553–54 (Jonathan Elliot ed.) (Lippincott 1836).

19 *Madison's Report on the Resolutions:* 4 *Elliot's Debates* 546–80.

19   *"Minority address" on the Resolutions:* Attributed to John Marshall in Albert J. Beveridge's 1919 *Life of John Marshall,* pp. 401–6. That attribution was persuasively challenged in an editor's note in 3 *The Papers of John Marshall* 499 (William C. Stinchcombe and Charles T. Cullen eds.) (1979). An extended note in 12 *The Papers of John Marshall* 512–524 (Charles F. Hobson ed.) (2006) shows conclusively that Henry Lee was the author and that in fact Marshall made it known that he would have opposed the Sedition Act had he been a member of the House when it was adopted.

20   *Jefferson's letter to Abigail Adams:* 1 *The Adams-Jefferson Letters: The Complete Correspondence Between Thomas Jefferson and Abigail and John Adams* 274–76 (Lester Capon ed.) (University of North Carolina Press 1959).

21   *Hofstadter:* Richard Hofstadter, Harper's, November 1964, p. 77.

21   *Madison's letter to Jefferson:* May 13, 1798.

Chapter 3

24   *Patterson case: Patterson v. Colorado,* 205 U.S. 454 (1907).

26   *Schenck case: Schenck v. United States,* 249 U.S. 47 (1919).

26   *Holmes: The Common Law* (Little, Brown 1881; Belknap Press of Harvard University Press 1963; Dover 1991).

27   *Frohwerk case: Frohwerk v. United States,* 249 U.S. 204 (1919).

27   *Debs case: Debs v. United States,* 249 U.S. 211 (1919).

28   *Abrams case: Abrams v. United States,* 250 U.S. 616 (1919). For a full account of the *Abrams* case and its participants, see Richard Polenberg, *Fighting Faiths: The Abrams Case, the Supreme Court and Free Speech* (Viking 1988).

30   *Masses case: Masses Publishing Co. v. Patten,* 244 F. 535 (S.D.N.Y. 1917).

30   *Hand-Holmes correspondence:* Gerald Gunther, *Learned Hand and the Origins of Modern First Amendment Doctrine: Some Fragments of History,* 27 Stanford L. Rev. 719 (1975).

31 *Chafee article:* Zechariah Chafee, *Freedom of Speech in War Time*, 32 Harvard L.R. 932 (1919).

31 *Holmes's letter to Chafee:* See David M. Rabban, *The Emergence of Modern First Amendment Doctrine*, 50 University of Chicago L. Rev. 1205, 1265–66, 1271 (1983).

33 *Acheson: Morning and Noon* 40 (Houghton Mifflin 1965).

34 *Gitlow case: Gitlow v. New York,* 268 U.S. 652 (1925).

35 *Statement by Hughes:* Charles Evans Hughes, *The Supreme Court of the United States* 68 (1928).

35 *Whitney case: Whitney v. California,* 274 U.S. 357 (1927). The Brandeis opinion starts on p. 374.

37 *Schwimmer case: United States v. Schwimmer,* 279 U.S. 644 (1929).

Chapter 4

39 *Stromberg case: Stromberg v. California,* 283 U.S. 359 (1931).

40 *Flag-burning case: Texas v. Johnson,* 491 U.S. 397 (1989).

41 *Holmes in 1920: Missouri v. Holland,* 252 U.S. 416 (1920).

41 *Hughes in 1934: Home Building and Loan Association v. Blaisdell,* 290 U.S. 398, 442–43 (1934).

42 *Black's comments:* Black joined the dissent in *Cohen v. California,* 403 U.S. 15 (1971).

43 *Near case: Near v. Minnesota,* 283 U.S. 697 (1931).

45 *Friendly: Minnesota Rag* (Random House 1981; Vintage 1982).

45 *Irving Shapiro's story:* Ibid., 40–42, 57–58.

46 *Grosjean case: Grosjean v. American Press Co.,* 297 U.S. 233 (1936).

47 *Pentagon Papers case: New York Times v. United States,* 403 U.S. 713 (1971). Justice Black's opinion in the case is at p. 717.

48 *King advertisement: New York Times Co. v. Sullivan,* 376 U.S. 254 (1964).

54 *Brennan lecture: The Meiklejohn Lecture,* 79 Harvard L.R. 1 (1965).

55 Bickel: *The Least Dangerous Politics: The Supreme Court at the Bar of Politics* 267 (Bobbs-Merrill 1963; Yale University Press 1986).

57 *Extension of the* Sullivan *rule to public figures:* See *Gertz v. Robert Welch Inc.*, 418 U.S. 323 (1974).

57 *Jefferson on the press:* Letter to J. Norvell, 1807.

58 *Russian criminal code:* News Alert, Committee to Protect Journalists (New York), July 28, 2006.

58 *Meiklejohn:* See Harry Kalven Jr., *The New York Times Case: A Note on "The Central Meaning of the First Amendment,"* 1964 Supreme Court Rev. 191, 221 n.125.

Chapter 5

59 *Sidis case: Sidis v. F-R Publishing Corporation,* 113 F.2d 806 (1940).

60 *Manley's article:* The New Yorker, Aug. 14, 1937, p. 22.

61 *Bok: Secrets: On the Ethics of Concealment and Revelation,* 250–52 (Pantheon 1983; Vintage 1984).

62 *Time, Inc. case: Time, Inc. v. Hill,* 385 U.S. 374 (1967).

64 *Schwartz: The Unpublished Opinions of the Warren Court* 251, 272 (Oxford University Press 1985).

67 *Garment article: Annals of Law: The Hill Case,* New Yorker, Apr. 17, 1989, p. 90.

68 *Brandeis-Warren article: The Right to Privacy,* 4 Harvard L.R. 193 (1890).

69 *Olmstead case: Olmstead v. United States,* 277 U.S. 438, 478 (Brandeis's dissent) (1928). *Olmstead* was overruled in *Katz v. United States,* 389 U.S. 347 (1967).

70 *Woody Allen case: Allen v. Men's World,* 15 Media Law Reporter 1001 (1988).

70 *Bette Midler case:* Decision of the United States Court of Appeals for the Ninth Circuit, marked not for publication, July 16, 1991.

70 *Jacqueline Onassis case: Onassis v. Dior,* 472 NYSupp 254 (1984).

70 *Shulman case: Shulman v. Group W,* 955 P.2d 469 (Cal. 1998).

72 *Sipple case: Sipple v. Chronicle Pub. Co.,* 201 Cal. Reporter 665 (Ct. App. 1984).

73 *Red Kimono case: Melvin v. Reid,* 297 Pac. 91 (Cal. App. 1931).

74 *Cox Broadcasting case: Cox Broadcasting v. Cohn,* 420 U.S. 469 (1975).

75 *Other cases involving confidentiality:* See *Landmark Communications v. Virginia,* 435 U.S. 29 (1978); *Smith v. Daily Mail Publishing Co.,* 443 U.S. 97 (1979); *Florida Star v. B.J.F.,* 491 U.S. 524 (1989).

75 *Telephone interception case: Bartnicki v. Vopper,* 532 U.S. 514 (2001).

77 *The English case:* A v. B Plc, 2 All E.R. 545.

78 *Nagel:* Thomas Nagel, *The Shredding of Public Privacy,* Times Literary Supplement, Aug. 14, 1998, p. 15.

79 *Kundera on the Prochazka case:* Milan Kundera, *Testaments Betrayed: An Essay in Nine Parts* (Harper Collins 1995).

79 *Kundera interview: A Talk with Milan Kundera,* New York Times Magazine, May 19, 1985, p. 85.

Chapter 6

81 *Judy Garland case: Garland v. Torre,* 259 F.2d 545 (2d Cir. 1958).

83 *Branzburg case: Branzburg v. Hayes,* 408 U.S. 665 (1972).

85 *Pentagon Papers case: New York Times v. United States,* 403 U.S. 713 (1971).

90 *Damages for disclosing a source: Cohen v. Cowles Media,* 501 U.S. 663 (1991).

91 *United States v. Wen Ho Lee:* Statement of Judge James A. Parker at sentencing, Sept. 13, 1990.

92 *Boston Globe editorial:* June 11, 2006.

93 *To the Point magazine:* Feb. 1, 1970.

93 *Buthelezi case: Buthelezi v. Poorter and Others* (1975), 4 So. Afr.L.R. 608.

95 *Farber decision in the New Jersey Supreme Court:* Matter of Farber, 78 N.J. 259 (1978).

97 *The closed courtroom decision: Richmond Newspapers v. Virginia,* 448 U.S. 555 (1980).

97 *Stewart lecture:* Lecture at Yale Law School, Nov. 2, 1974, reprinted in 26 Hastings L.J. 631 (1975).

98 *Congressional act of 1975:* Rule 501 of the Federal Rules of Evidence.

98 *Tatel's comments:* Judge Tatel explained his proposal in a concurring opinion in *In re Grand Jury Subpoena,* 397 F.3d 964, 986 (D.C. Cir. 2005).

99 *Joseph Wilson on Niger: What I Didn't Find in Africa,* New York Times, July 6, 2003, Sect. 4, p. 9, col. 1.

100 *Justice Brennan:* Address, 32 Rutgers L.R. 173 (1979).

Chapter 7

105 *Charles Evans Hughes:* See Clemens P. Work, *Darkest Before Dawn* 240 (University of New Mexico Press, 2005).

105 *Burleson:* Ibid., 10.

106 *Emma Goldman:* This comment appears in her autobiography, Emma Goldman, *Living My Life,* vol. 2, 704 (Dover Edition 1970).

108 *Gitlow case: Gitlow v. New York,* 268 U.S. 652 (1925).

109 *De Jonge case: De Jonge v. Oregon,* 299 U.S. 353 (1937).

110 *Herndon case: Herndon v. Lowry,* 301 U.S. 242 (1937).

111 *Cantwell case: Cantwell v. Connecticut,* 310 U.S. 296 (1940).

113 *Korematsu case: Korematsu v. United States,* 323 U.S. 214 (1944).

114 *Minersville case: Minersville School District v. Gobitis,* 310 U.S. 586 (1940).

114 *West Virginia case: West Virginia Board of Education v. Barnette,* 319 U.S. 624 (1943).

115 *License plate case: Wooley v. Maynard,* 430 U.S. 705 (1977).

116 *Barenblatt case: Barenblatt v. United States,* 360 U.S. 109 (1959).

117 *Sweezy case: Sweezy v. New Hampshire,* 354 U.S. 234 (1957).

119 *Wiecek's comment on the security screening process:* William M. Wiecek, *The Birth of the Modern Constitution: The United States Supreme Court, 1941–53,* vol. 12 of *The Oliver Wendell Holmes Devise History of the Supreme Court of the United States,* at 583 (Cambridge University Press 2006).

120 *Dennis case: Dennis v. United States,* 341 U.S. 494 (1951). The Second Circuit decision in *Dennis v. United States:* 183 F.2d 201 (1950).

121 *Redish article:* 73 U.Cin.L.R. 9 (2004).

122 *"Homer nodded":* Learned Hand, *The Bill of Rights: The Oliver Wendell Holmes Lectures* 59 (1958; Harvard University Press 1962).

122 *"Prosecuted those birds":* Geoffrey R. Stone, *Perilous Times: Free Speech in Wartime, from the Sedition Act of 1798 to the War on Terrorism* 395 (W.W. Norton 2004).

123 *Yates case: Yates v. United States,* 354 U.S. 298 (1957).

123 *Scales case: Scales v. United States,* 367 U.S. 203 (1961).

124 *Brandenburg case: Brandenburg v. Ohio,* 395 U.S. 444 (1969).

124 *Lamont case: Lamont v. Postmaster General,* 381 U.S. 301 (1965).

125 *"These bums":* Richard Nixon, remarks to Pentagon employees in informal conversation, May 1, 1970.

126 *Bond case: Bond v. Floyd,* 385 U.S. 116 (1966).

128 *Wheeler's statement:* Work, *Darkest Before Dawn* 113.

129 *Judge Bourquin:* Ibid., 118.

130 *Knauff case: Knauff v. Shaughnessy,* 338 U.S. 537 (1950).

Chapter 8

131 *Cohen case: Cohen v. California,* 403 U.S. 15, 24–25 (1971). The transcript of the argument is found in 70 *Landmark Briefs and Arguments of the Supreme Court of the United States: Constitutional Law* 828 (P. Kurland and G. Casper eds. 1975).

133 *Woolsey's opinion: United States v. One Book called "Ulysses,"* 5 F.Supp. 182 (S.D.N.Y. 1933).

133 *Hecate County case: Doubleday & Co. v. New York,* 335 U.S. 848 (1948).

133 *Roth case: Roth v. United States,* 354 U.S. 476 (1957).

135 *Burstyn case: Burstyn v. Wilson,* 343 U.S. 495 (1952).

136 *Jacobellis case: in Jacobellis v. Ohio,* 378 U.S. 184, 197 (1964).

136 *Justice Brennan's "utterly without redeeming social value": Memoirs v. Massachusetts,* 383 U.S. 413, 418 (1966).

136 *Court withdrew that requirement:* The test was rejected in *Miller v. California,* 413 U.S. 15 (1973), Brennan dissenting.

136 *Bork's argument:* Robert H. Bork, *Neutral Principles and Some First Amendment Problems,* 47 Indiana L.J. 1 (1971).

137 *Adult zoning case: City of Renton v. Playtime Theatres,* 475 U.S. 41 (1986).

137 *"Seven dirty words" case: FCC v. Pacifica Foundation,* 438 U.S. 726 (1978).

138 *MacKinnon: Only Words* (Harvard University Press 1993).

138 *Indianapolis case: American Booksellers Association v. Hudnut,* 771 F.2d 323 (1985).

138 *Meese commission:* Final Report of the Attorney General's Commission on Pornography, 1986.

138 *Hustler case: Hustler v. Falwell,* 485 U.S. 46 (1988).

140 *Ginsberg's "Howl":* Judge Horn's unpublished opinion was handed down on Oct. 3, 1957. See Bill Morgan and Nancy Peters (eds.), *Howl on Trial: The Battle for Free Expression* 198 (City Lights Books 2006). See also Ronald Collins and David Skover, *Mania: The Madcap Stories of the Lives That Launched a Nation* (Sourcebooks Forthcoming), Part 4.

Chapter 9

146 *Madison:* Report on the Virginia Resolutions.

148 *The alien sweep:* See Anthony Lewis, *Un-American Activities,* review of David Cole, *Enemy Aliens: Double Standards and*

Constitutional Freedoms in the War on Terrorism, New York Review of Books, Oct. 23, 2003, p. 16.

149 *"Patchouli girls":* Hank Stuever, *The Art of Peace: Deploying Posters and Body Paint, the Anti-Warriors,* Washington Post, Jan. 20, 2003, p. C1.

149 *Edgar and Schmidt:* Harold Edgar and Benno Schmidt Jr., *Espionage Statutes and the Publication of Defense Information,* 73 Columbia L.R. 929 (1973).

150 *Ashcroft comment:* New York Times, Dec. 7, 2001, p. 1, col. 4.

151 *Bush wiretapping:* James Risen and Eric Lichtblau of the *Times* wrote many stories on NSA wiretapping starting on Dec. 16, 2005, p. A1, col. 1, with *Bush Lets U.S. Spy on Callers without Courts.* Their Pulitzer Prize: See New York Times, Apr. 18, 2006, p. B7, col. 1.

152 *Harman case: Home Office v. Harman,* [1983] 1 A.C. 280.

153 *Bridges case: Bridges v. California,* 314 U.S. 252 (1941).

Chapter 10

158 *Beauharnais case: Beauharnais v. Illinois,* 343 U.S. 250 (1952).

159 *Skokie case: Collin v. Smith,* 578 F.2d 1197 (1978).

160 *The Economist:* Oct. 21, 2006, p. 64.

161 *Irving and Lipstadt:* See New York Times, Dec. 21, 2006, p. A3, col. 1.

161 *"You are attacking . . . "* See New York Times, Aug. 21, 2006, p. A8, col. 1.

162 *"Praiseworthy":* See New York Times, Feb. 9, 2007, p. A11, col. 1.

162 *Waldron:* See London Review of Books, July 20, 2006, pages 22–23.

165 *Flag-burning case: Texas v. Johnson,* 491 U.S. 397 (1989).

165 *Second flag-burning case: United States v. Eichman,* 496 U.S. 310 (1990).

166 *Rwanda:* See Stephen Kinzer, *Big Gamble in Rwanda,* New York Review of Books, Mar. 29, 2007, p. 23.

Chapter 11

170 *David Berkowitz:* See "Caught," New York Post, Aug. 11, 1977, p. 1. Berkowitz was convicted of six murders and sentenced, for each, to twenty-five years to life. See also New York Times, June 13, 1978, A1, col. 5.

171 *Irvin case: Irvin v. Dowd,* 359 U.S. 394 (1959).

172 *Sheppard decision: Sheppard v. Maxwell,* 384 U.S. 333 (1966).

174 *Nebraska case: Nebraska Press Association v. Stuart,* 427 U.S. 539 (1976).

175 *Gannett case: Gannett Co. v. DePasquale,* 443 U.S. 368 (1979).

176 *Richmond case: Richmond Newspapers v. Virginia,* 448 U.S. 555 (1980).

177 *Buckley case: Buckley v. Valeo,* 424 U.S. 1 (1976).

178 *2002 campaign reform law:* Bipartisan Campaign Reform Act of 2002.

178 *The decision upholding the law: McConnell v. Federal Election Commission,* 540 U.S. 93 (2003).

178 *The decision on the reform act: Federal Election Commission v. Wisconsin Right to Life* see New York Times, June 26, 2007, p. A1: "Justices Loosen Ad Restrictions in Campaign Law," by Linda Greenhouse and David Kirkpatrick.

179 *Republican Party case: Republican Party of Minnesota v. White,* 536 U.S. 765 (2002).

180 *Hughes:* Charles Evans Hughes, *The Supreme Court of the United States* 68 (Columbia University Press 1928).

180 *Dred Scott case: Dred Scott v. Sanford,* 60 U.S. 393 (1857).

181 *Legal tender case:* The first of the legal tender cases was *Hepburn v. Griswold,* 75 U.S. 603 (1869).

181 *The income tax case: Pollock v. Farmers' Loan & Trust Co.,* 157 U.S. 429 (1895).

181   *Lawrence case: Lawrence v. Texas*, 539 U.S. 558 (2003).

181   *Roe v. Wade*, 410 U.S. 113 (1973).

Chapter 12

183   *Samuel Adams:* Speech in Philadelphia, Aug. 1, 1776.

183   *Chafee:* Zechariah Chafee Jr., *Free Speech in the United States* 33 (Harvard University Press 1941).

184   *Einstein:* Walter Isaacson, *Einstein* 480 (Simon & Schuster 2007); see also note 26.

185   *Blasi:* Vincent Blasi, *Holmes and the Marketplace of Ideas,* Supreme Court Rev. 2004, 1, 39.

186   *Meiklejohn:* Alexander Meiklejohn, *Free Speech and Its Relation to Self-Government* (Harper Brothers 1948).

187   *"We are very quiet there":* Oliver Wendell Holmes Jr., "Law and the Court," speech, Feb. 15, 1913.

187   *Brown case:* 347 U.S. 483 (1954).

189   *Durr on Black:* Virginia Foster Durr, *Outside the Magic Circle* 167 (University of Alabama Press 1985; Simon & Schuster/ Touchstone 1987).

189   *Nur Fatima:* See New York Times, Sept. 10, 2006, p. A1.

INDEX

ABC News, 92
Abortion, 179, 180
Abrams, Jacob, 37
Abrams v. United States, 28–29, 32, 33, 35, 37, 43, 103, 185
Abu Ghraib prison, 151
Abuse of power, 89–90, 151, 185
Academic freedom, 118
Acheson, Dean, 33
ACLU. *See* American Civil Liberties Union
Adams, Abigail, 12, 20, 103–104
Adams, John, x, 5, 7, 11, 14, 15, 18, 20, 52, 179
Adams, Samuel, 183, 189
Ahmet, Atilla, 161
Alabama, 49, 50
Allen, John, 16
Allen, Woody, 70
American Civil Liberties Union (ACLU), 107, 160, 178
American Newspaper Publishers Association, 176
American Tragedy, An (Dreiser), 133

Anti-Semitism, 43, 44, 104, 124, 166
Ashcroft, John, 150
Associated Press, 92
Association of American Editorial Cartoonists, 139
Austen, Jane, 141

Bailey, Dorothy, 119–120
Baltimore American, 13
Barak, Aharon, xii
Barenblatt v. United States, 116
Bartnicki v. Vopper, 75
Beauharnais v. Illinois, 158–159
Berger, Victor, 105
Berkowitz, David, 170–171
Berman, Howard, 164–165
Bernstein, Carl, 56
Bickel, Alexander M., 55
Bill of rights, 7, 8, 9, 23
Bin Laden, Osama, 150–151
Black, Hugo L., 42–43, 47–48, 49, 54, 65, 116–117, 122, 134, 135, 153, 154–155, 158, 189
Blackmun, Harry, 175

Blackstone, Sir William, 3, 6, 16, 44
Blasi, Vincent, 57, 185, 186
Bloggers, 85, 91, 147
Bok, Derek, 85
Bok, Sissela, 61, 62
Bolam, Silvester, 170
Bolshevik Revolution, 28, 104
Bond v. Floyd, 126
Bork, Robert H., 136–137
Boroff, Phil, 70
Boston Globe, 92–93
Boston Independent Chronicle, 13
Bourquin, George M., 129–130
Brandeis, Louis D., 28, 44, 46, 53, 68–69, 71, 76, 79, 105, 107, 108, 162, 180, 184, 186–187, 188. *See also* Supreme Court, dissenting opinions of Holmes and Brandeis
Brandenburg v. Ohio, 124, 159, 162
Branzburg v. Hayes, 83–88, 91, 98
Brennan, William J., Jr., 52, 53–54, 54–55, 66–67, 100, 133–134, 136, 165, 166
Breyer, Stephen, 76
Bribery, 52–53
Bridges v. California, 153–155, 171
Britain, ix, xi, xii, xiii, 1, 6, 17, 19, 24, 46, 50, 77–78, 140, 145, 161, 166
House of Lords, 55

pretrial comments by media in, 169–170
Queen's bedroom in Buckingham Palace entered, 143–144, 170
See also Press, British vs. American
Brown v. Board of Education, 48, 187, 188
Buckley v. Valeo, 177
Burden of proof, 50, 55
Burger, Warren E., 115, 131, 174
Burleson, Albert, 105, 122
Burstyn v. Wilson, 135
Bush, George W., 19, 21, 89, 99, 127, 128
powers asserted by, 148, 149, 151, 186
Buthelezi, Reverend Dr. Manas, 93
Butler, Pierce, 45
Byrne, Brendan, 95
Byrnes, James F., 155
Byron (Lord), 164

Caen, Herb, 72
California's Criminal Syndicalism Act, 105
Callender, James T., 14, 15
Cambodia, 126
Campari, 139
Campbell, Will, 102
Canadian Supreme Court, 157–158
Cantwell v. Connecticut, 111–112

Carlin, George, 137
CBS television, 81–83
Censorship, 2, 133, 134, 138,
   141, 164. *See also* Prior
   restraint
Chafee, Zechariah, Jr., 31, 107,
   183–184
Chase, Samuel, 14, 15
Checks and balances, 128, 147
Chicago Seven, 125
Chicago Tribune, 44
CIA, 127
Citizenship, 180–181
Civil rights movement, 48, 51, 55
Clark, Charles, 60, 73, 77
Clark, Tom C., 67, 135, 172–173
Clear and present danger,
   concept of, 26, 27, 28, 31,
   108, 120–121, 122, 171, 174,
   187
Clinton, Bill, 77
Cohen v. California, 42, 131–132,
   138
Cointelpro, 188
Cold War, 115, 119
Common law, xi, 3, 4, 7, 19, 50,
   98, 155
Common Law, The (Holmes), 26
Communism, 21, 54, 79, 104,
   115, 118, 124, 188
   being soft on communism, 119
Communist Labor Party of
   California, 35, 184
Communist Party, 109, 110,
   120, 121

Constitution, 6–7, 17, 32, 113,
   128, 166–167
   changing interpretation of, x,
   9. *See also* First Amendment,
   defining words of
   and common-law practice, 7
   constitutional democracy,
   xii–xiii
   original intent of Framers, 9,
   40–41, 42, 154
   ratification of, 7–8
Contempt of congress, 116
Contempt of court, 90, 92, 152,
   153, 172
Cooper, Matt, 99, 100
Cosby, William, 4
Courage, 128–129, 147, 156,
   186–187, 188
Courier-Journal of Louisville,
   Kentucky, 83
Cox Broadcasting v. Cohn, 74
Criminal syndicalism, 35,
   104–105, 109
Croswell, Harry, 5–6, 14
Czechoslovakia, 79

Daily Mirror (London), 170
*Darkest Before Dawn: Sedition and
   Free Speech in the American
   West* (Work), 102, 103, 129
Death penalty, 2, 4
Debs, Eugene, 127
   Debs v. United States, 27,
      29–30, 31, 126
De Jonge v. Oregon, 109–110, 111

Democratic Party, 12, 56, 119, 125

Denning (Lord), 142

Dennis v. United States, 120–122, 124

Desperate Hours, The (play) 63

Detention of American citizens indefinitely, 127, 128

Dickens, Charles, 143

"Dissertation on the Canon and Feudal Law, A" (J. Adams), 18

Doctor Zhivago (Pasternak), 184

Douglas, William O., 54, 87, 122, 125, 134–135

Dred Scott case, 180–181

Dreiser, Theodore, 133

Due process, 24, 119. *See also* Fourteenth Amendment

Durr, Virginia, 189

Dyer, Mary, 4

Economist, The, 160–161

Edgar, Harold, 149

Einstein, Albert, 184

Election of 1800, xv, 12, 15, 188

Elliott, Andrea, 189

Emergence of a Free Press (Levy), 5

Enemy combatants, 21, 89, 148

Errera, Roger, 160

Espionage Act of 1917, 25–28, 103, 105. *See also Abrams v. United States*

European Convention on Human Rights, xiii, 153

European Court of Human Rights, xiii–xiv

Fagan, Michael, 143

Fallaci, Oriana, 161

Falwell, Jerry, 138–139, 159

Farber, Myron, 95

Fatima, Nur, 189

FCC. *See* Federal Communications Commission

Fear, use of, 21, 103–104, 112, 118, 127, 128, 150, 189

Federal Communications Commission (FCC), 137, 140

Federal government, 146–147

Federalism, 17

Federalist Party, 11, 14, 15–16

Ferlinghetti, Lawrence, 140

Films, 73, 135, 138, 140, 145, 172

First Amendment
  birth of, 6, 9, 10
  and compelling speech, 114–115
  and courtrooms being closed, 175–176
  defining words of, 39–40. *See also* Constitution, original intent of Framers
  and false statements, 43, 54. *See also Near v. Minnesota*
  federal law in violation of, 125

and Fourteenth Amendment,
25, 35, 44, 109
and freedom of assembly,
109–110
informing purpose of, 51
legislative investigation as
violating, 117
and privacy, 62–68, 71, 72, 80.
See also Privacy
protection of individual and
social interests, 183–185
and right to a fair trial,
169–177
and symbolic speech, 40, 43,
165
Flag-burning, 40, 42, 165–166
Flag Protection Act of 1989,
165–166
Flag salute, 114, 123
Ford, Gerald R., 72
Fortas, Abe, 64–65, 67, 69
Fourteenth Amendment, 24, 175,
181. *See also under* First
Amendment
Fourth Amendment, 69
France, xiii
French Revolution, 12, 103,
119
Frankfurter, Felix, 38, 117–118,
154, 155, 158, 159
"Freedom of Speech in War
Time" (Chafee), 31
Freund, Paul A., 178
Friendly, Fred, 45, 46
Frohwerk v. United States, 27

Front Page, The (play), 145
Fugitive, The (film), 172

Gag orders, 174
Galileo, 184
Gallatin, Albert, 16
Gannett Co. v. DePasquale,
175–176
Garland, Judy, 81–83, 86–87
Garment, Leonard, 67–68
Geneva Conventions, 127
German language, 102
Germany, xiii, 104, 115, 157
Ginsberg, Allen, 140
Ginsburg, Ruth Bader, xiv
Gitlow v. New York, 34–35,
108–109
Goldberg, Arthur, 54
Goldman, Emma, 106
Goodale, James, 51
Government employees, 118–120
Graham, Katharine, 56, 147
Grand juries, 83, 85, 86, 90, 129
Greenfield, Edward J., 70
Grosjean v. American Press Co., 46
Guantanamo Bay, Cuba, 127

Habeas corpus petition, 129, 173
Haigh, John George, 170
Hall, Grover C., Jr., 51
Hamilton, Andrew, 4
Hancock, John, 8
Hand, Learned, 30–31, 53, 107,
120—121, 122, 124
Harding, Warren G., 127

Harlan, John Marshall (the
    elder), 25
Harlan, John Marshall (the
    younger), 67, 68, 116, 117,
    123, 132, 135
Harman, Harriet, 152
Harvard Law Review, 31, 68
Hate speech, 157–167
    on university campuses,
    163–164
Helena Independent, 102
Henry, Patrick, 8
Henry VIII, 1
Herndon v. Lowry, 110–111
Heroin, 88, 89
Hill, James, 63. *See also Time, Inc.
    v. Hill*
Hiss, Alger, 172
Hitler, Adolf, 160
Hoaxes, 88–89
Hoffman, Julius, 125
Hollywood Ten, 116
Holmes, Oliver Wendell, Jr., xiv,
    24, 25–38, 43, 103, 107, 108,
    119, 122, 124, 180, 183, 185
    and original intent of Framers
    of Constitution, 41
    wife of, 33
Holocaust deniers, 157, 158, 161
Homosexuality, 72, 181, 187
Hoover, J. Edgar, 121, 188
Horn, Clayton W., 140
House Committee on Un-
    American Activities,
    115–116

"Howl" (Ginsberg), 140
Hughes, Charles Evans, x, 35, 39,
    41–42, 44–45, 46–47, 105,
    107, 109, 154
    on damaging Supreme Court
    decisions, 180–181
Hussein, Saddam, 148
Hustler v. Falwell, 138–139, 159
Hutus, 166

Illinois, 158, 159–160
Income tax, 181
India, xiii
Indianapolis, 138
Indonesia, 58
International Studies in Higher
    Education Act, 164
Internet. *See* Bloggers
Intrusion (as branch of privacy
    law), 70–71
Iraq War, xv, 19, 27, 148–149,
    165, 186, 189
Irving, David, 161
Islam, 161
IWW. *See* Workers of the
    World
Izzadeen, Abu, 162

Jackson, Janet, 140
Jackson, Robert H., 113, 114,
    130, 155, 164
Jacobellis v. Ohio, 136
Japanese Americans, relocation
    of, 112–113, 127, 188
Jascalevich, Dr. Mario, 95

Jefferson, Thomas, 5, 8–9, 12, 14, 15, 57–58
Jeffersonian newspapers, 13
and Sedition Act of 1798, 20, 52, 106
Jehovah's Witness, 111, 114, 115
Jennison, Nathaniel, 7
John, Elton, 145
Johnson, Gregory Lee, 165
Johnson, Lyndon B., 56, 125
Jones, Walter B., 49, 51
Joyce, James, 133, 141
Judiciary, xii, xiv, xv, 2, 9, 13, 49, 187–188
elections of judges, 178–180
judicial activism, x, 188
See also Supreme Court
Juries, 169, 173, 175, 176, 177

Kemal Ataturk, 58
Kennedy, John F., 56, 123, 124, 173
Kennedy, Robert, 124
Kent State University, 126
Kentucky, 17
King, Martin Luther, Jr., 48, 49, 50, 51
Kirkland, Weymouth, 44
Knauff, Ellen, 130
Know-Nothing Party, 104
Korematsu v. United States, 113
Ku Klux Klan, 124, 159
Kundera, Milan, 79–80

Lachowsky, Hyman, 37. *See also Abrams v. United States*
Lady Chatterley's Lover (Lawrence), 132
Lamont v. Postmaster General, 124–125
Lawrence, D. H., 132, 141
Lawrence v. Texas, 181
Lee, Henry (Light Horse Harry), 19–20
Lee, Wen Ho, 91–93
Legacy of Suppression (Levy), 5
Legal tender cases of 1869, 181
Leggett, Vanessa, 90–91
Levin, Bernard, 145–146, 156
Levy, Leonard, 5
Lewinsky, Monica, 77
Libby, Lewis, 99
Libel, xiii, 46, 48, 51, 55, 66, 134, 144
"three galloping presumptions" of libel law, 50
See also New York Times v. Sullivan; Seditious libel
Liberty Bonds, 113
Licensing system for publications, 1–2, 3, 6, 91
Life magazine, 63. *See also Time, Inc. v. Hill*
Lingens, Peter Michael, xiii
Lipman, Samuel, 37. *See also Abrams v. United States*
Lippmann, Walter, 125
Lipstadt, Deborah, 161
Long, Huey, 46

Look-alikes, 70
Los Angeles Times, 92, 153
Lovejoy, Elijah Parish, 158
Loyalty programs, 118–120
Lyon, Matthew, 13–14, 20

McCarthy, Joseph, 21, 54, 104, 118, 119, 123
McCormick, Robert Rutherford, 44, 45
MacKinnon, Catharine, 138
Madison, James, xii, 21, 40, 44, 52–53, 56
  and bill of rights, 8, 9, 10
  on duty of the press, 146, 186
  Madisonian premise, 18, 21
  and Sedition Act of 1798, 17–19, 106
Malaysia, 58
Manley, Jared L., 60, 61
Marbury v. Madison, 9
Marketplace of ideas, 185
Markham, James E., 44
Marshall, George C., 54
Marshall, John, 9, 23, 84, 188
Martin Chuzzlewit (Dickens), 143
Mason, George, 8
Mason, Stevens T., 14
Massachusetts, 7, 8, 179
Masses, The (magazine), 30, 122
Masses Publishing Co. v. Patten, 30
Meese, Edwin L., 138
Meiklejohn, Alexander, 68, 186
Mein Kampf (Hitler), 160
Melvin v. Reid, 73

Memoirs of Hecate County (Wilson), 133
Mencken, H. L, 138
Midler, Bette, 70
Mill, John Stuart, 184–185
Miller, Judith, 99, 100
Milton, John, 2, 3
Minersville School District v. Gobitis, 114
Minnesota, 43, 179, 180
Minnesota Rag (Friendly), 45
Miracle, The (film), 135, 138
Montana state sedition law, 101–103, 128–129
Montgomery Advertiser, 51
Moore, Sara Jane, 72
Morning and Noon (Acheson), 33
Morrison, Stanley, 33
Murphy, Frank, 113

Nagel, Thomas, 78
Nast, Thomas, 139
National Rifle Association, 178
National security, 18, 147
National Security Agency, 89
Nazis, 157, 159–160, 163
Near, Jay M., 43, 45–46
  Near v. Minnesota, 44–47, 48, 96
Nebraska Press Association v. Stuart, 174
Nebraska Supreme Court, 174
Newbold, David M., 185
New Deal, 146
New Hampshire, 115, 117

New York (state), 6, 8, 105
New York Argus, 13
New Yorker, The, 60, 61, 68
New York Herald Tribune, 81
New York Post, 170–171
New York Society for the
    Suppression of Vice, 133
New York Times, 18, 53, 59, 86,
    87, 89, 92, 95, 99, 147, 149,
    150, 151, 185, 189
    New York Times v. Sullivan, 17,
        48–58, 62, 66, 96, 134, 139,
        155, 159, 181
    *New York Times v. United
        States*, 47–48
    rules for confidentiality at, 96
New York Weekly Journal, 4–5
Nicholas, John, 16–17, 54
Niger, 99
Nimmer, Melville, B., 131
Nixon, Richard M., 18, 21, 47,
    56, 64, 67–68, 84, 85,
    125–126
Nobel Prize, 184
Novak, Robert, 99

Obscenity, 133–134, 135, 136
O'Connor, Sandra Day, 76
Olmstead v. United States, 69
Omnibus Crime Control and
    Safe Streets Act of 1968, 75
Onassis, Jacqueline Kennedy, 70
"On Liberty" (Mill), 185
Oregon's criminal syndicalism
    law, 109

Originalists. *See* Constitution,
    original intent of Framers
Oswald, Lee Harvey, 173
Our Gal Friday (film), 145

Pakistan, 58
Palmer Raids, 106, 188
Paper money, 181
Pardons, 102, 127
Pasternak, Boris, 184
Paterson, William, 13, 15
Patterson, John, 51
Patterson v. Colorado, 24, 26
Pentagon Papers, 18, 47, 56, 85,
    147, 149
Permanent Investigations
    Subcommittee, 118
Philadelphia Aurora, 5, 13
Pickering, Timothy, 13
Plea bargaining, 175
Police misconduct, 175
Political campaign financing,
    177–178
Political cartoons, 139
Political correctness, 164
Popkin, Samuel, 85
Pornography, 136, 137, 138, 140,
    141
Powell, Lewis F., Jr., 87–88
Press, 128
    British vs. American, 143–145,
        152, 154, 155
    duty of, 146, 186
    and pretrial publicity,
        171–174

Press *(continued)*
after September 11, 2001,
147–151
See also Testimonial privilege
Prior restraint, 2, 3, 5, 6, 16, 24,
44, 46–47, 48, 96, 174
Privacy, 59–80, 117
of conversations, 75–76
false light privacy, 63–64,
69–70
four branches of privacy law,
63–64, 69–73
as the right to be let alone, 65,
68–69
state statutes requiring
confidentiality, 74–75
See also under First Amendment
Prochazka, Jan, 79
Progressive Party, 117
Property rights, 24
Public figures, 57, 60, 61, 62, 73
Pulitzer Prize, 88, 151
Punitive damages, 179
Puritans, 3–4

Quakers, 38

Racism, 48, 49, 55, 119, 158, 162,
187. *See also* Hate speech
Rape victims, 74–75
Reagan, Ronald, 127, 137, 165
Red Channels magazine, 116
Redish, Martin H., 121
Red Kimono The (film), 73
Red Scares, 104, 115, 122–123

Rehnquist, William H., 139
Reid, Richard, 166
Religion, 1, 3–4, 38, 114, 129,
161. *See also* Roman
Catholic Church
Republican Party, 56, 119, 179
National Convention of 1984,
165
Republican Party (original), 12,
17
Reston, James B., 125
Reynolds, Barbara, 70
Rice, Condoleezza, 150
Richmond Examiner, 13
Richmond Newspapers v. Virginia,
176
"Right to Privacy, The" (Brandeis
and S. Warren), 68–69
Roberts, Owen J., 111–112, 113
Roe v. Wade, 180, 181
Roman Catholic Church, 104,
111–112, 184
Roosevelt, Franklin D., 112, 118,
146, 155
Roth v. United States, 133, 135,
136
Ruby, Jack, 173
Russia, 28, 58, 104. *See also* Soviet
Union
Rwanda, 166

Sanford, Edward T., 109
San Francisco Chronicle, 72
Saturday Press (Minnesota), 43, 44
Scales, Junius, 123–124

Scalia, Antonin, 42, 139
Schenck v. United States, 26, 27
Schmidt, Benno, Jr., 149
Schwartz, Bernard, 64, 67
Schweitzer, Brian, 102
Schwimmer, Rosika, 37
Secrecy, 128, 189
Secrets (Bok), 61
Sedition Act of 1798, 11–21, 52,
    106
  found unconstitutional, 53
Sedition Act of 1918, 103, 105
  repeal of, 127
Seditious libel, 2, 3, 4, 24, 58
  truth as defense concerning, 6,
    13
  See also Montana state sedition
    law; Sedition Act of 1798;
    Sedition Act of 1918
September 11, 2001, terrorist
    attacks, 127, 148, 150
Sermon on the Mount, 38
Sexism, 119
Sexuality, 132, 134, 135, 137,
    138, 139
Shapiro, Irving, 45–46
Sheppard v. Maxwell, 172–173
Shield laws, 91, 93. *See also*
    Testimonial privilege
Shulman v. Group W Productions,
    70–72, 73
Sidis, William James, 59–60
  *Sidis v. F-R Publishing
    Corporation*, 60–62, 71, 73,
    77

Simants, Erwin Charles, 174
Sipple, Oliver S., 72
Sixteenth Amendment, 181
Sixth Amendment, 175
Skokie, Illinois, 159–160, 163
Slavery, 7, 158
Smith Act, 123–124
Socialist Party, 27, 105, 126
Sodomy, 181
Son of Sam, 170–171
South Africa, xiii, 93–94
Soviet Union, 121, 124, 149. *See
    also* Cold War; Russia
Speech codes, 163–164. *See also*
    Censorship
"Spirit of Liberty, The" (Hand),
    107
Stanford University, 163
Starr, Kenneth, 77
Steimer, Mollie, 28, 37. *See also
    Abrams v. United States*
Stevens, John Paul, 76, 176
Stewart, Potter, 52, 82–83,
    86–87, 97, 98, 136, 147, 175
Stewart, Sam, 102
Stone, Harlan F., 114
Story, Joseph, 45
Stromberg v. California, 39, 40
Student Nonviolent
    Coordinating Committee,
    126
Suicide bombers, 161–162, 166.
    See also Terrorism
Sullivan, L. B., 49. *See also New
    York Times v. Sullivan*

Sulzberger, Arthur Ochs, 147
Sun, The, 140, 144
Sunday People, 143–144, 170
Superbowl game of 2004, 140
Supreme Court, xii, 15, 94, 98,
    187
  damaging decisions of, 180–181
  dissenting opinions of Holmes
    and Brandeis, 28–29, 32, 34,
    35–38, 185
  first dissenting support of First
    Amendment, 23
  first majority support of First
    Amendment, 39
  and press privilege claims, 87,
    96
Sutherland, George, 46
Swastika, 157, 159
Swaziland, 58
Sweezy, Paul, 117

Talk radio, 57
Tammany Hall, 139
Taney, Roger, B., 180
Tatel, David, 98, 100
Taylor, Telford, 123
Terrorism, 12, 127–128, 161–162,
    166–167. *See also* September
    11, 2001, terrorist attacks
Testimonial privilege, 82, 83, 87,
    88, 94, 96
  and defendants in criminal
    prosecutions, 94–95
  defining who is entitled to,
    84–85, 91

  and public policy, 97–98
  qualified privilege for
    journalists, 98, 99, 100
Texas v. Johnson, 40
Thurber, James, 61, 62
Time, Inc. v. Hill, 62–68, 69, 71
  and suicide of Mrs. Hill, 68
Time magazine, 99
Times, The (London), 145
Torre, Marie, 81–83, 86–87
Torture, 127, 128, 186
To the Point magazine, 93
Tribe, Laurence, 176
Truman, Harry S., 118, 119, 120
Truth, 184–185
Turkey, 58
Tutsis, 166
Tweed, Boss, 139

Ulysses (Joyce), 133, 138
United States v. Eichman,
    165–166
United States v. Schwimmer, 37–38
Unnamed informers, 119–120
*Unpublished Opinions of the Warren
    Court, The* (Schwartz), 64,
    67–68
Uranium ore, 99

Van Devanter, Willis, 111
Venona documents, 121
Vermont Journal, 13
Vietnam War, 18, 27, 42, 47, 56,
    125–126, 132, 149
Vinson, Fred M., 121

Virginia, 8, 9
  Declaration of Rights adopted
    in legislature, 6, 7
  Virginia Resolutions of James
    Madison, 17–18, 19
Voting Rights Act of 1965, 56

Waldron, Clarence, 103
Waldron, Jeremy, 162–163
Walker, Quock, 7
Wallace, Amy, 60
Warren, Earl, 64, 67, 112–113,
    126, 173
Warren, Samuel D., 68, 69, 76
Washington, Bushrod, 15
Washington, George, 5, 6, 139,
    147
Washington Post, 56, 88, 92, 147,
    148–149
Wasp, The, 5
Watergate, 56, 84, 89–90, 147,
    149, 151
Wechsler, Herbert, 52
Werdegar, Kathryn M., 71–72, 73
*West Virginia Board of Education v.
    Barnette*, 114, 123
Wheeler, Burton K., 128–129
White, Byron R., 74, 83–86, 88, 91

Whitney v. California, 35–37, 105,
    162, 184, 186
Wiecek, William M., 119
Wilson, Edmund, 133
Wilson, Joseph and Valerie
    Plame, 99
Wilson, Woodrow, x, 25, 28, 103,
    105
Wiretapping, 19, 69, 79, 89, 99,
    127, 128, 151, 186
Woodward, Bob, 56
Woolf (Lord Chief Justice),
    77–78
Woolsey, John M., 133, 138
Work, Clemens P., 102, 129
Workers of the World (IWW),
    104
World War I, 25, 27, 101, 113,
    126, 128–129, 155
World War II, 112. *See also*
    Japanese Americans,
    relocation of

Yates v. United States, 123
Young, C. C., 36–37

Zenger, John Peter, 4
Zoning laws, 137